J

F

$10.00

# This is your PASSBOOK for

# BLUEPRINTER

CITY · STATE · FEDERAL

## QUESTIONS & ANSWERS

*CIVIL SERVICE DIVISION*
NATIONAL LEARNING CORPORATION

C-1621
ISBN 0-8373-1621-9

THE PASSBOOK[R] SERIES

PASSBOOKS[R]

FOR

CAREER OPPORTUNITIES

BLUEPRINTER

NATIONAL LEARNING CORPORATION

20 DuPont Street                     Plainview, New York 11803

516/935-5800

C-1621
ISBN 0-8373-1621-9

THE PASSBOOK® SERIES

PASSBOOKS®

# BLUEPRINTER

NATIONAL LEARNING CORPORATION

20 DuPont Street                    Plainview, New York 11803

516/935-5800

# PASSBOOK SERIES ®

The *PASSBOOK SERIES* has been created to prepare applicants and candidates for the ultimate academic battlefield — the examination room.

At some time in our lives, each and every one of us may be required to take an examination — for validation, matriculation, admission, qualification, registration, certification, or licensure.

Based on the assumption that every applicant or candidate has met the basic formal educational standards, has taken the required number of courses, and read the necessary texts, the *PASSBOOK SERIES* furnishes the one special preparation which may assure passing with confidence, instead of failing with insecurity. Examination questions — together with answers — are furnished as the basic vehicle for study so that the mysteries of the examination and its compounding difficulties may be eliminated or diminished by a sure method.

This book is meant to help you pass your examination provided that you qualify and are serious in your objective.

The entire field is reviewed through the huge store of content information which is succinctly presented through a provocative and challenging approach — the question-and-answer method.

A climate of success is established by furnishing the correct answers at the end of each test.

You soon learn to recognize types of questions, forms of questions, and patterns of questioning. You may even begin to anticipate expected outcomes.

You perceive that many questions are repeated or adapted so that you gain acute insights, which may enable you to score many sure points.

You learn how to confront new questions, or types of questions, and to attack them confidently and work out the correct answers.

You note objectives and emphases, and recognize pitfalls and dangers, so that you may make positive educational adjustments.

Moreover, you are kept fully informed in relation to new concepts, methods, practices, and directions in the field.

You discover that you are actually taking the examination all the time: you are preparing for the examination by "taking" an examination, not by reading extraneous and/or supererogatory textbooks.

In short, this PASSBOOK, used directedly, should be an important factor in helping you to pass your test.

# EXAMINATION SECTION

# CONTENTS

———

# EXAMINATION SECTION

# C O N T E N T S

—

# EXAMINATION SECTION

# C O N T E N T S

—

# EXAMINATION SECTION

# C O N T E N T S

—

# C O N T E N T S

## ABSTRACT REASONING

———

# BASIC FUNDAMENTALS OF BLUEPRINT READING

# HOW TO TAKE A TEST

You have studied hard, long, and conscientiously.

With your official admission card in hand, and your heart pounding, you have been admitted to the examination room.

You note that there are several hundred other applicants in the examination room waiting to take the same test.

They all appear to be equally well prepared.

You know that nothing but your best effort will suffice. The "moment of truth" is at hand: you now have to demonstrate objectively, in writing, your knowledge of content and your understanding of subject matter.

You are fighting the most important battle of your life -- to pass and/or score high on an examination which will determine your career and provide the economic basis for your livelihood.

What extra, special things should you know and should you do in taking the examination?

## BEFORE THE TEST

YOUR PHYSICAL CONDITION IS IMPORTANT

If you are not well, you can't do your best work on tests. If you are half asleep, you can't do your best either. Here are some tips:
1. Get about the same amount of sleep you usually get. Don't stay up all night before the test, either partying or worrying -- DON'T DO IT.
2. If you wear glasses, be sure to wear them when you go to take the test. This goes for hearing aids, too.
3. If you have any physical problems that may keep you from doing your best, be sure to tell the person giving the test. If you are sick or in poor health, you really cannot do your best on any test. You can always come back and take the test some other time.

## AT THE TEST

EXAMINATION TECHNIQUES

1. Read the *general* instructions carefully. These are usually printed on the first page of the examination booklet. As a rule, these instructions refer to the timing of the examination; the fact that you should not start work until the signal and must stop work at a signal, etc. If there are any *special* instructions, such as a choice of questions to be answered, make sure that you note this instruction carefully.

2. When you are ready to start work on the examination, that is as soon as the signal has been given, read the instructions to each question booklet, underline any key words or phrases, such as *least, best, outline, describe,* and the like. In this way you will tend to answer as requested rather than discover on reviewing your paper that you *listed without describing,* that you selected the *worst* choice rather than the *best* choice, etc.

3. If the examination is of the objective or so-called multiple-choice type, that is, each question will also give a series of possible answers: A,B,C, or D, and you are called upon to select the best answer and write the letter next to that answer on your answer paper, it is advisable to start answering each question in turn. There may be anywhere from 50 to 100 such questions in the three or four hours allotted and you can see how much time would be taken if you read through all the questions before beginning to answer any. Furthermore, if you come across a question or a group of questions which you know would be difficult to answer, it would undoubtedly affect your handling of all the other questions.

4. If the examination is of the essay-type and contains but a few questions, it is a moot point as to whether you should read all the questions before starting to answer any one. Of course if you are given a choice, say five out of seven and the like, then it is essential to read all the questions so you can eliminate the two which are most difficult. If, however, you are asked to answer all the questions, there may be danger in trying to answer the easiest one first because you may find that you will spend too much time on it. The best technique is to answer the first question, then proceed to the second, etc.

5. Time your answers. Before the examination begins, write down the time it started, then add the time allowed for the examination and write down the time it must be completed, then divide the time available somewhat as follows:
   a. If 3 1/2 hours are allowed, that would be 210 minutes. If you have 80 objective-type questions, that would be an average of about 2 1/2 minutes per question. Allow yourself no more than 2 minutes per question, or a total of 160 minutes, which will permit about 50 minutes to review.
   b. If for the time allotment of 210 minutes, there are 7 essay questions to answer, that would average about 30 minutes a question. Give yourself only 25 minutes per question so that you have about 35 minutes to review.

6. The most important instruction is *to read each question* and make sure you know what is wanted. The second most important instruction is to *time yourself·properly* so that you answer every question. The third most important instruction is to *answer every question*. Guess if you have to but include something for each question. Remember that you will receive no credit for a blank and will probably receive some credit if you write something in answer to an essay question. If you guess a letter, say "B" for a multiple-choice question, you may have guessed right. If you leave a blank as the answer to a multiple-choice question, the examiners may respect your feelings but it will not add a point to your score.

7. Suggestions
   a. Objective-Type Questions
      (1) Examine the question booklet for proper sequence of pages and questions.
      (2) Read all instructions carefully.
      (3) Skip any question which seems too difficult; return to it after all other questions have been answered.
      (4) Apportion your time properly; do not spend too much time on any single question or group of questions.
      (5) Note and underline key words -- *all, most, fewest, least, best, worst, same, opposite.*
      (6) Pay particular attention to negatives.
      (7) Note unusual option, e.g., unduly long, short, complex, different or similar in content to the body of the question.
      (8) Observe the use of "hedging" words - *probably, may, most likely, etc.*
      (9) Make sure that your answer is put next to the same number as the question.
      10) Do not second guess unless you have good reason to believe the second answer is definitely more correct.
      (11) Cross out original answer if you decide another answer is more accurate; do not erase.
      (12) Answer all questions; guess unless instructed otherwise.
      (13) Leave time for review.

   b. Essay-Type Questions
      (1) Read each question carefully.
      (2) Determine exactly what is wanted. Underline key words or phrases.
      (3) Decide on outline or paragraph answer.
      (4) Include many different points and elements unless asked to develop any one or two points or elements.
      (5) Show impartiality by giving pros and cons unless directed to select one side only.
      (6) Make and write down any assumptions you find necessary to answer the question.
      (7) Watch your English, grammar, punctuation, choice of words.
      (8) Time your answers; don't crowd material.

3

8. Answering the Essay Question

Most essay questions can be answered by framing the specific response around several key words or ideas. Here are a few such key words or ideas:

M's: manpower, materials, methods, money, management

P's: purpose, program, policy, plan, procedure, practice, problems, pitfalls, personnel, public relations

a. Six basic steps in handling problems:
    (1) preliminary plan and background development
    (2) collect information, data and facts
    (3) analyze and interpret information, data and facts
    (4) analyze and develop solutions as well as make recommendations
    (5) prepare report and sell recommendations
    (6) install recommendations and follow up effectiveness

b. Pitfalls to Avoid
    (1 *Taking things for granted*
        A statement of the situation does not necessarily imply that each of the elements is necessarily true; for example, a complaint may be invalid and biased so that all that can be taken for granted is that a complaint has been registered.
    (2) *Considering only one side of a situation*
        Wherever possible, indicate several alternatives and then point out the reasons you selected the best one.
    (3) *Failing to indicate follow up*
        Whenever your answer indicates action on your part, make certain that you will take proper follow-up action to see how successful your recommendations, procedures, or actions turn out to be.
    (4) *Taking too long in answering any single question*
        Remember to time your answers properly.

# EXAMINATION SECTION

# TEST

# 1

# TEST 1

DIRECTIONS: Directly and concisely, using brief answer form, answer the following questions.

1. What do you call another paper that will give the same results as Bruning's B-W?

2. What type of carbons do you use with DC current?

3. What are the names of the two MOST common blueprinting machines?

4. What are the five standard widths of blueprint paper?

5. What do you call the device used to regulate the speed of a blueprint machine?

6. Why don't Ozalid prints shrink or become brittle?

7. What prints are made by the following steps: exposure, fresh-water wash, hypo wash, fresh-water wash, and drying?

8. What do you call it when the coating on sensitized paper runs?

9. If the printing speed of the lamps is too fast for certain tracings, what should you do?

10. What do you call the process which produces a print that is direct, positive, permanent, and true to scale?

---

# KEY (CORRECT ANSWERS)

1. Ozalid
   Director (Dietzgen)
   Black-line (Post B-W)

2. Solid

3. Pease
   Revolute (Paragon)

4. 24; 30; 36; 42; 48; 54

5. Rheostat

6. Developed dry (no water used)
   Developed by fumes (developed by ammonia)

7. Van Dyke (negative)(brown-line)

8. Bleeding

9. Use (drop) shade
   Use (drop) shield
   Use (drop) curtain
   Use (drop) shutter

10. Ozalid
    B-W (black and white) (black-line)
    Direct

# TEST
# 2

TEST 2

DIRECTIONS: Directly and concisely, using brief answer form, answer the
following questions.

1. What happens to the background of Ozalid and Directo prints, if you run
the machine too fast?

2. What solution develops, preserves, or fixes Van Dykes and "brown-lines"?

3. How can you tell when there is too much air in the carbon lamp?

4. When completely finished, what is the color an overexposed blueprint?

5. What do you call the prints that are developed dry?

6. What happens to the background of a blueprint if you run the machine too fast?

7. What do you call the print that is developed with ammonia fumes?

8. What do you call the apparatus that gives the BEST contact for printing?

9. What do you call the roll of paper which draws the sensitized paper through
the machine?

10. What do you call the solution used in developing a blueprint?

———

# KEY (CORRECT ANSWERS)

1. Dirty (smudgy) (spotty) (streaked)
   Dark (gray) (black) (fogged)
   Too much
   Discolors

2. Hypo (sodium hyposulphite)

3. Foggy (smoky) (black) globe
   Arc flickers (jumps)
   Reddish (yellow) colored flame

4. Dark (deep) blue
   Slate blue
   Purple
   Dark

5. Ozalid (red-line)
   B-W (black and white) (black-line)

6. Light (white) (pale)
   Underexposed

7. Ozalid (red-line)

8. Vacuum frame (vacuum)

9. Leader

10. Potash (potassium bichromate)

TEST
3

# TEST 3

DIRECTIONS: Directly and concisely, using brief answer form, answer the
following questions.

1. What do you call the prints that give the LEAST shrinkage?

2. Why should you turn off the lights before you turn off the motor?

3. What do you call the process of checking the lights and putting in new carbons?

4. What prints are made by the following steps: exposure, fresh-water wash,
potash wash, water wash, and drying?

5. What is the FIRST thing you should do to make a "blue-line" from a regular
tracing?

6. What device regulates exposure without changing speed?

7. In what kind of prints do you MOST often find bleeding?

8. What do you call prints that have white lines on a dark brown background?

9. In "blue-line" prints, what part of the drawing does the light go through?

10. After a blueprint is completely finished, what is the color if the print has been
overexposed?

———

# KEY (CORRECT ANSWERS)

1. Ozalid;
   B-W (black and white) (black-line)
   Direct
   Vapor

2. Cool lights (cool cylinder)
   Keep lamps (glass) (cylinder) from breaking
   Remove heat

3. Trimming

4. Blueprints
   Blue-line prints

5. Make a Van Dyke (make a negative)

6. Shade (shutter) (damper) (curtain) (shield) (blind)

7. Blue-lines (white prints)

8. Van Dykes (negatives)

9. Lines (white part)

10. Dark (deep) blue
    Slate blue
    Purple
    Dark

# EXAMINATION SECTION

# TEST 1

DIRECTIONS: Each question or incomplete statement is followed by several suggested answers or completions. Select the one that *BEST* answers the question or completes the statement. *PRINT THE LETTER OF THE CORRECT ANSWER IN THE SPACE AT THE RIGHT.*

1. The plate on a photo-offset machine is *MOST LIKELY* to wear down as a result of incorrect pressure adjustment on the
    A. ductor rollers
    B. oscillating roller
    C. fountain roller
    D. ink-form rollers

    1.___

2. Suppose you are called away from your photo-offset press and you leave it running. While you are away, the paper stops feeding into the machine. When you return, which of the following should you do after turning off the machine and checking the feeding mechanisms?
    A. Check the ejector wheels    B. Wash the blanket
    C. Check the pickup roller    D. Adjust the ink flow

    2.___

3. The first job in the morning on a photo-offset machine always produces copies that are dirty and with tone. What is the problem?
    A. The dampener roller is dry.
    B. The night latch is off.    C. The blanket is tacky.
    D. There is too much drier in the ink.

    3.___

4. If the first 15 sheets printed on a photo-offset machine have a double image on one-half of the sheet, which of the following parts is *MOST* likely to be causing the trouble? The
    A. blanket
    B. master cylinder
    C. feed rollers
    D. impression cylinder

    4.___

5. To prevent double images after making vertical adjustments on a photo-offset machine, you *MUST*
    A. wash the blanket
    B. check the ink
    C. add water
    D. use a new plate

    5.___

6. When changing from 80-pound index stock to 20-pound bond stock on the photo-offset machine, you must change the sheet detector *and* the
    A. ink       B. water       C. impression    D. blanket

    6.___

7. Emulsification is *MOST* likely to occur when
    A. pigment is mixed with the ink
    B. excessive water rides with the ink
    C. there is excessive ink on the printed sheet
    D. the inking form or plate rollers are set improperly

    7.___

8. For proper functioning of a photo-offset machine, new water rollers and new blankets *MUST* be
    A. loosened   B. pulled      C. soaked       D. run in

    8.___

9. Suppose that a photo-offset machine operator who is in      9.___
   the process of running a "big job" is called away for an
   hour and must stop the machine.  Under these circumstances,
   which of the following is the *BEST* action for the operator
   to take in order to assure that the printed material will
   be satisfactory?
   A. Wash the blanket before leaving
   B. Gum the plate before leaving
   C. Add water when restarting   D. Add ink when restarting

10. Suppose that more copies of a complex drawing are required 10.___
    and everything but the old plate has been destroyed.
    Which of the following is the *BEST* way to reproduce the
    drawing?
    A. Put the plate on the press without any preparation
    B. Process the plate as if it had just been exposed
    C. Gum the plate before using it
    D. Wash the plate with fountain solution

11. If an operator is printing a 3.000-copy run on a photo-    11.___
    offset machine and the copy begins to wash out, he should
    *FIRST* check the
    A. ink and water          B. ink blade
    C. vibrator roller        D. impression cylinder

12. The person who arranges negatives into flats is called    12.___
    a(n)
    A. artist     B. stripper     C. cameraman   D. platemaker

13. When the night latch is engaged upon first starting a     13.___
    photo-offset machine, which rollers will *NOT* have ink?
    The
    A. ductor rollers         B. idler rollers
    C. water rollers          D. feed rollers

14. Assume that an operator has just completed a job on index 14.___
    stock on a photo-offset machine.  However, when he tries
    to print the next job on 20-pound mimeograph paper, there
    is no image.  What is *MOST LIKELY* to be the problem?
    A. The feed is loose.      B. There is no impression.
    C. The blanket is loose.
    D. The ink rollers are not properly aligned.

15. While printing card stock on a Multilith, an operator     15.___
    finds that the suction feet jam on the pull-out rollers.
    Of the following, the *MOST* likely reason for this is that
    A. the feet and the pull-out rollers are too close
       together
    B. the machine is running at too slow a speed
    C. the card stock is too thick for the machine
    D. there is a curl in the card stock

16. The pull-in rollers on the Multilith are usually set at   16.___
    an even tension, but sometimes it is necessary to have more
    tension on one than on the other, depending on the stock
    being used.  The need for uneven tension is *MOST LIKELY*
    to occur when the stock being printed is
    A. coated stock           B. onion skin (tissue)
    C. bond paper             D. No. 10 envelopes

17. After cleaning the cylinder on an A.B. Dick 350 (Direct      17.___
    Delivery) machine, you start printing on 8 1/2" x 11"
    paper and find that the paper sticks and jams before going
    into the tray. This is *MOST LIKELY* to be caused by
    A. gum on the stock
    B. improper functioning of the blower and vacuum
    C. the ejector rollers being out of alignment
    D. a break in the static line

18. Suppose that after 25 copies of a 100-copy job are printed 18.___
    on a photo-offset machine, the image breaks down. After
    making certain that the pressure on the dampener rollers
    is correct, the operator should *THEN* check the
    A. stop fingers
    B. condition of the paper stock
    C. plate-to-blanket pressure
    D. upper and lower feed rollers

19. Of the following, the *MOST* economical way to proof a four- 19.___
    color process job is to
    A. use positive prints      B. use a color key
    C. run process plates       D. run the key color only

20. When conventional fountain solution is being mixed, the     20.___
    *MAXIMUM* amount of gum arabic per gallon of water that
    should be used is
    A. 1/4 ounce  B. 1 ounce      C. 2 ounces   D. 2 1/4 ounces

21. The *PURPOSE* of the separator fingers on a photo-offset     21.___
    machine is to
    A. push the paper on to the registration board
    B. prevent more than one sheet from feeding at the same
       time
    C. place a sheet of paper on top of each printed sheet
       as it comes off the press
    D. separate the printed sheets into lots of 100

22. On a photo-offset machine, what roller receives ink         22.___
    *DIRECTLY* from the ink fountain?  The
    A. idler roller           B. ink form roller
    C. ink ductor roller      D. water roller

23. On both offset duplicator and cylinder presses, the one     23.___
    of the following parts which has grippers is the
    A. impression cylinder    B. plate cylinder
    C. suction feet           D. friction feed

24. A registration board is a part of each of the following     24.___
    offset presses *EXCEPT* the
    A. Davidson 600           B. Chief 15
    C. Multilith 1250         D. A.B. Dick 350

25. The image area of a lithographic plate *MUST* be            25.___
    A. hydrophilic            B. embossed
    C. hydrophobic            D. desensitized

4. (#1)

KEY (CORRECT ANSWERS)

| | | | | |
|---|---|---|---|---|
| 1. | D | | 11. | A |
| 2. | B | | 12. | B |
| 3. | A | | 13. | C |
| 4. | A | | 14. | B |
| 5. | A | | 15. | A |
| | | | | |
| 6. | C | | 16. | D |
| 7. | B | | 17. | C |
| 8. | D | | 18. | C |
| 9. | B | | 19. | B |
| 10. | B | | 20. | B |

| | |
|---|---|
| 21. | B |
| 22. | C |
| 23. | A |
| 24. | D |
| 25. | C |

———

DIRECTIONS:   Each question or incomplete statement is followed by
                several suggested answers or completions.  Select the
                one that *BEST* answers the question or completes the
                statement.  *PRINT THE LETTER OF THE CORRECT ANSWER IN
                THE SPACE AT THE RIGHT.*

1.  In order to obtain an exact reproduction of black-and-          1.____
    white typed copy with diagrams, it would be *BEST* to use a
        A. mimeograph machine        B. Xerox machine
        C. hectograph machine        D. Rexograph machine

2.  On the photo-offset machine, the static line is located        2.____
    *BETWEEN* the
        A. stop fingers and the feed rollers
        B. ejector plate and the upper ejector wheels
        C. impression roller and the ejector plate
        D. ejector rings and the paper receiver

3.  The Aquamatic system is part of which of the following         3.____
    machines?
        A. Multilith   B. Chief 17   C. A.B. Dick   D. Davidson 600

4.  The *PURPOSE* of the jogger operation is to                    4.____
        A. feed paper                B. maintain registration
        C. retain the paper          D. lower the image

5.  The *PURPOSE* of the fountain solution is to                   5.____
        A. prevent oxidation of both image and non-image areas
           of the plate
        B. dampen the plate and keep non-printing areas from
           accepting ink
        C. regulate the flow of ink to prevent flooding the
           blanket with ink
        D. prevent stripping of image and non-image areas
           of the plate

6.  The speed of a web offset press is expressed in terms of       6.____
        A. sheets per hour           B. feet per minute
        C. impressions per hour      D. impressions per minute

7.  Which one of the following printing processes reproduces       7.____
    illustrations in continuous tone?
        A. Mimeograph                B. Photogelatin or Collotype
        C. Thermography              D. Xerography

8.  How many cylinders does a Ditto machine have?                  8.____
        A. ONe        B. Two        C. Three        D. Four

9.  For reproduction by most printing processes, continuous        9.____
    tone images
        A. must be converted into a line image
        B. must be in black and white
        C. must be converted into halftones
        D. cannot be printed with a different type of image

10. The gripper edge of the paper is the                      10.___
    A. jogger edge             B. tail edge
    C. side edge              D. leading edge

11. The *PREFERRED* side for printing on bond paper is the      11.___
    A. felt side  B. wire side   C. coated side  D. rough side

12. What is the *GREATEST* problem of the operator while learn-  12.___
    ing to run an offset press?
    A. Avoiding blackouts
    B. Obtaining the proper ink and water balance
    C. Feeding sheets into the press
    D. Oiling the press

13. After the A.B. Dick 350 or 360 has been loaded, paper will  13.___
    not rise into the feeding area unless which of the follow-
    ing parts of the machine is in the proper place?
    A. Table release       B. Paper guide crank
    C. Feed table           D. Operator lever

14. The scale measurement on an offset press is *USUALLY* in     14.___
    A. sixteenths of an inch   B. eighths of an inch
    C. half inches          D. inches

15. When comparing the photo-negative method of preparing       15.___
    offset masters with dye-transfer, infrared and diffusion-
    transfer methods, the photo-negative method is *SUPERIOR*
    in that
    A. it costs less money to prepare the master
    B. it is a simpler method
    C. the operation takes less time
    D. the image may be enlarged or reduced

16. Paper printing plates are classified as                     16.___
    A. wipe-on plates       B. subtractive plates
    C. direct-image plates    D. two-sided plates

17. Which of the following should be used to mark guidelines    17.___
    on a paste-up?  A(n)
    A. #2 pencil          B. ball point pen
    C. embossing pen       D. light blue pencil

18. The ITEK machine is used to make                            18.___
    A. plates              B. negatives
    C. positives           D. black and white copies

19. The *MAXIMUM* number of acceptable copies that can be ob-    19.___
    tained from a spirit master usually falls within the range
    of
    A. 100-150    B. 200-500     C. 600-1000    D. 1100-1500

20. The color of the light that is *BEST* for a plate room and   20.___
    is *FREE* of ultraviolet rays is
    A. red        B. black     C. yellow     D. blue

21. The one of the following substances that is used to        21.___
    prepare plates with presensitized and wipe on plate
    coatings is
       A. Diazo sensitizer       B. ammonium dichromate
       C. lacquer               D. gum arabic

22. If excessive scumming occurs on additive plates after      22.___
    they have been gummed, what is *MOST LIKELY* to be the cause?
       A. Subtractive gum was used.
       B. The gum was polished dry with a disposable wipe.
       C. Image developer was not used.
       D. Desensitizer was used.

23. Suppose you are told to print a year's supply of a form.   23.___
    If 1500 copies are used each month and the form is printed
    three up on an 8 1/2" x 14" sheet and cut to 4 1/2" x 8 1/2",
    how many 8 1/2" x 14" sheets are needed (disregarding
    waste)?
       A. 3,000     B. 4,500     C. 5,400     D. 6,000

24. The *MAXIMUM* number of 4" x 5" pieces that can be cut      24.___
    from five 500-sheet packages of 16" x 21" paper is
       A. 30,000    B. 40,000    C. 50,000    D. 60,000

25. The type of ink used on a mimeograph machine is            25.___
       A. solid             B. semi-solid
       C. fluid             D. heat-set

# KEY (CORRECT ANSWERS)

| | | | | |
|---|---|---|---|---|
| 1. | B | | 11. | A |
| 2. | D | | 12. | B |
| 3. | C | | 13. | A |
| 4. | B | | 14. | B |
| 5. | B | | 15. | D |
| | | | | |
| 6. | B | | 16. | C |
| 7. | B | | 17. | D |
| 8. | A | | 18. | A |
| 9. | C | | 19. | A |
| 10. | D | | 20. | C |

| | |
|---|---|
| 21. | A |
| 22. | A |
| 23. | D |
| 24. | B |
| 25. | C |

TEST 3

DIRECTIONS: Each question or incomplete statement is followed by several suggested answers or completions. Select the one that *BEST* answers the question or completes the statement. *PRINT THE LETTER OF THE CORRECT ANSWER IN THE SPACE AT THE RIGHT.*

1. Stripped negatives are held in place by
   A. lithograph tape
   B. staples
   C. rubber cement
   D. masking tape

1.___

2. The maximum number of 3" x 5" pieces that can be cut from one sheet of 17" x 22" paper is
   A. 20
   B. 21
   C. 22
   D. 23

2.___

3. The size of a number 10 envelope is
   A. 4 1/8" x 9 1/2"
   B. 5" x 9"
   C. 4" x 6 1/4"
   D. 3" x 5"

3.___

4. A printing process that uses a toner instead of ink is called
   A. presensitized
   B. wipe-on
   C. electrostatic
   D. long-run

4.___

5. An additive plate *DIFFERS* from a subtractive plate in that an additive plate
   A. is color coated on both sides
   B. is color coated on one side
   C. is not color coated at all
   D. has a red or green side

5.___

6. Normally, in order to determine if a line plate is sufficiently exposed, the transparent numbered platemaker's 1/2" x 5" twenty-one step gray scale should develop to a solid step
   A. 20 or 21
   B. 18 or 19
   C. 5 or 6
   D. 1 or 2

6.___

7. Currently, the metal *MOST WIDELY* used in making plates for offset printing presses is
   A. zinc
   B. aluminum
   C. copper
   D. tin

7.___

8. Assume that you are responsible for ordering supplies for the duplicating section in your agency. Which one of the following actions would be most helpful in determining when to place orders so that an adequate supply of materials will be on hand at all times?
   A. Taking an inventory of supplies on hand at least every two months
   B. Asking your subordinates to inform you when they see that supplies are low
   C. Checking the inventory of supplies whenever you have time
   D. Keeping a running inventory of supplies and a record of estimated needs

8.___

9. When ordering or taking inventory of supplies for the       9.___
   duplicating section, the one of the following items which
   you should consider to be *LEAST* important is
   A. paper                      B. ink
   C. deletion fluid             D. gum arabic

Questions 10 - 14.

DIRECTIONS: Answer questions 10 through 14 *SOLELY* on the basis of
           the following chart.

### DUPLICATION JOBS

| JOB NO. | DATES Submitted 1974 | DATES Required 1974 | DATES Completed 1974 | PROCESS | NO. OF ORIGINALS | NO. OF COPIES OF EACH ORIGINAL | REQUEST-ING UNIT |
|---|---|---|---|---|---|---|---|
| 324 | 6/22 | 6/25 | 6/25 | Xerox | 14 | 25 | Research |
| 325 | 6/25 | 6/27 | 6/28 | Mimeo-graph | 10 | 125 | Training |
| 326 | 6/25 | 6/25 | 6/25 | Xerox | 12 | 11 | Budget |
| 327 | 6/25 | 6/27 | 6/26 | Multi-lith | 17 | 775 | Admin. Div. H |
| 328 | 6/28 | ASAP* | 6/25 | Multi-lith | 5 | 535 | Personnel |
| 329 | 6/26 | 6/26 | 6/27 | Xerox | 15 | 8 | Admin. Div. G |

*ASAP - As soon as possible.

10. The unit whose job was to be xeroxed but was *NOT* completed 10.___
    by the date required is
    A. Admin. Div. H            B. Admin. Div. G
    C. Research                 D. Training

11. The job with the *LARGEST* number of original pages to be    11.___
    xeroxed is job number
    A. 324      B. 326      C. 327      D. 329

12. Jobs were completed *AFTER* June 26, 1974 for               12.___
    A. Training and Admin. Div. G
    B. Training and Admin. Div. H
    C. Research and Budget      D. Admin. Div. G only

13. Which one of the following units submitted a job which    13.____
    was completed *SOONER* than required?
        A. Training                 B. Admin. Div. H
        C. Personnel                D. Admin. Div. G

14. The jobs which were submitted on different days but were   14.____
    completed on the *SAME* day and used the *SAME* process had
    Job Numbers
        A. 324 and 326              B. 327 and 328
        C. 324, 326 and 328         D. 324, 326 and 329

Questions 15 - 17.

DIRECTIONS: Answer questions 15 through 17 *SOLELY* on the basis of
            the information contained in the following paragraph.

    Suppose you are given the job of printing, collating and stapling
8,000 copies of a 10 page booklet as soon as possible. You have available one photo-offset machine, a collator with an automatic stapler,
and the personnel to operate these machines. All will be available
for however long the job takes to complete. The photo-offset machine
prints 5,000 impressions an hour, and it takes about 15 minutes to set
up a plate. The collator, including time for insertion of pages and
stapling, can process about 2,000 booklets an hour. (Answers should
be based on the assumption that there are no breakdowns or delays.)

15. Assuming that all the printing is finished before the     15.____
    collating is started, if the job is given to you late
    Monday and your section can begin work the next day and is
    able to devote seven hours a day, Monday through Friday,
    to the job until it is finished, what is the *BEST* estimate
    of when the job will be finished?
        A. Wednesday afternoon of the same week
        B. Thursday morning of the same week
        C. Friday morning of the same week
        D. Monday morning of the next week

16. An operator suggests to you that instead of completing     16.____
    all the printing and then beginning collating and stapling,
    you first print all the pages for 4,000 booklets, so that
    they can be collated and stapled while the last 4,000
    booklets are being printed. If you accepted this suggestion,
    the job would be completed
        A. sooner but would require more man-hours
        B. at the same time using either method
        C. later and would require more man-hours
        D. sooner but there would be more wear and tear on the
           plates

17. Assume that you have the same assignment and equipment as   17.____
    described above, but 16,000 copies of the booklet are
    needed instead of 8,000. If you decided to print 8,000
    complete booklets, then collate and staple them while you
    started printing the next 8,000 booklets, which of the
    following statements would *MOST* accurately describe the

relationship between this new method, and your original
method of printing all the booklets at one time, and
then collating and stapling them?
- A. The job would be completed at the same time regard-
less of the method used.
- B. The new method would result in the job's being completed 3 1/2 hours earlier.
- C. The original method would result in the job's being
completed an hour later.
- D. The new method would result in the job's being
completed 1 1/2 hours earlier.

18. If a supervisor of a duplicating section in an agency          18.____
hears a rumor concerning a change in agency personnel
policy through the "grapevine," he should
- A. repeat it to his subordinates so they will be informed
- B. not repeat it to his subordinates before he determines the facts because, as supervisor, his word may
give it unwarranted authority
- C. repeat it to his subordinates so that they will like
him for confiding in them
- D. not repeat it to his subordinates before he determines
the facts because a duplicating section is not concerned with matters of policy

19. When teaching a new employee how to operate a press, a          19.____
supervisor should *FIRST*
- A. let the employee try to operate the machine by him-
self, since he can learn only by his mistakes
- B. explain the process to him with the use of diagrams
before showing him the machine
- C. have him memorize the details of the operation from
the manual
- D. explain and demonstrate the various steps in the
process, making sure he understands each step

20. If a subordinate accuses you of always giving him the          20.____
least desirable assignments, you should *IMMEDIATELY*
- A. tell him that it is not true and you do not want to
hear any more about it
- B. try to get specific details from him, so that you can
find out what his impressions are based on
- C. tell him that you distribute assignments in the
fairest way possible and he must be mistaken
- D. ask him what current assignment he has that he does
not like, and assign it to someone else

21. Suppose that the production of an operator under your          21.____
supervision has been unsatisfactory and you have decided
to have a talk with him about it. During the interview,
it would be *BEST* for you, as his supervisor, to
- A. discuss only the subordinate's weak points so that
he can overcome them
- B. discuss only the subordinate's strong points so that
he will not become discouraged
- C. compare the subordinate's work with that of his co-
workers so that he will know what is expected of him
- D. discuss both his weak and strong points so that he

22. Suppose that an operator under your supervision makes a    22.___
    mistake in color on a 2,000-page job and runs it on
    white paper instead of on blue paper. Of the following,
    your *BEST* course in these circumstances would be to
    point out the error to the operator and
    A. have the operator rerun the job immediately on blue
       paper
    B. send the job to the person who ordered it without
       comment
    C. send the job to the person who ordered it and tell
       him it could not be done on blue paper
    D. ask the person who ordered the job whether the white
       paper is acceptable

23. Assuming that all your subordinates have equal technical   23.___
    competence, the *BEST* policy for a supervisor to follow
    when making assignments of undesirable jobs would be to
    A. distribute them as evenly as possible among his
       subordinates
    B. give them to the subordinate with the poorest
       attendance record
    C. ask the subordinate with the least seniority to do them
    D. assign them to the subordinate who is least likely
       to complain

24. To get the *BEST* results when training a number of sub-   24.___
    ordinates at the same time, a supervisor should
    A. treat all of them in an identical manner to avoid
       accusations of favoritism
    B. treat them all fairly, but use different approaches
       in dealing with people of different personality types
    C. train only one subordinate, and have him train the
       others, because this will save a lot of the super-
       visor's time
    D. train first the subordinates who learn quickly so as to
       make the others think that the operation is easy to
       learn

25. After putting a new employee under your supervision        25.___
    through an initial training period, assigning him to work
    with a more experienced employee for a while would be a
    A. *good idea*, because it would give him the opportunity
       to observe what he had been taught and to participate
       in production himself
    B. *bad idea*, because he should not be required to work
       under the direction of anyone who is not his super-
       visor
    C. *good idea*, because it would raise the morale of the
       more experienced employee who could use him to do
       all the unpleasant chores
    D. *bad idea*, because the best way for him to learn would
       be to give him full responsibility for assignments
       right away

___ (#3)

# KEY (CORRECT ANSWERS)

| | | | | |
|---|---|---|---|---|
| 1. | A | | 11. | D |
| 2. | B | | 12. | A |
| 3. | A | | 13. | B |
| 4. | C | | 14. | A |
| 5. | C | | 15. | C |
| | | | | |
| 6. | C | | 16. | C |
| 7. | B | | 17. | D |
| 8. | D | | 18. | B |
| 9. | C | | 19. | D |
| 10. | B | | 20. | B |

| | |
|---|---|
| 21. | D |
| 22. | D |
| 23. | A |
| 24. | B |
| 25. | A |

————

# EXAMINATION SECTION

TEST 1

DIRECTIONS: Directly and concisely, using brief answer form, answer the
following questions.

1. What will happen if you have too much carbonate in the developer?

2. When the pointers on the camera bed and the leg are at 200, what will be
the size of the photocopy?

3. What has happened to the developing agent in a developing solution if it
turns brown?

4. What chemical prevents rapid oxidation of the developer when in contact
with the air?

5. In order to align the prism, with what do you line up the cross hair on the
ground glass?

6. How long do you develop a regular negative print at room temperature?

7. On which photocopying machine is the paper wound with the emulsion side out?

8. How do you set the diaphragm when using ground glass to get a focus?

9. At what temperature should you keep developers containing hydroquinone in
order to insure maximum contrast?

10. What make of photocopy machine develops prints in a spiral tank?

———

## KEY (CORRECT ANSWERS)

1. Fogs
   Develops too fast
   Softens emulsion
   Increases contrast

2. Double (twice)
   100% larger

3. Oxidized
   Weakened (exhausted) (deteriorated)

4. Sulphite (sodium sulphite) (hypo)

5. Cross (center) of board
   Cross (center) of book holder
   Center of copy (center of object)

6. 40 seconds to 1 minute

7. Photostat

8. Open

9. 70 degrees to 75 degrees

10. Rectigraph

# TEST 2

DIRECTIONS: Directly and concisely, using brief answer form, answer the following questions.

1. What do you remove from the photocopy apparatus to make a negative in reverse?

2. What happens to the prints if the hypo becomes alkaline?

3. If a lot of developer is carried over to the hypo solution, what kind of hypo bath should be used?

4. On which photocopying machine is the paper wound with the emulsion side in?

5. What chemical in the developer helps to restrain fog?

6. What is the MOST COMMON acid which may be used in the potassium alum bath?

7. What do you call the part of the machine that holds the paper?

8. After cutting, in what position should you leave the lever which controls the knife blade?

9. With what kind of negatives do you use number one paper?

10. What happens if you leave prints in the hypo too long?

———

## KEY (CORRECT ANSWERS)

1. Prism

2. Stain (turn yellow) (turn brown)
   Spot
   Fog (fade)

3. Acid (acetic)

4. Rectigraph

5. Bromide (potassium bromide)

6. Acetic

7. Magazine
   Box (paper box)

8. Up and down (vertical) (up)
   Back (original)

9. Contrasty (contrasting)
   Hard
   Dense
   Strong
   Heavy

10. Bleach
    Fade

# EXAMINATION SECTION

# TEST 1

DIRECTIONS: Directly and concisely, using brief answer form, answer the following questions.

1. Underneath which rollers are the paper fingers found?

2. What may you use to thin the ink?

3. What holds the paper down on the conveyor?

4. How many "grippers" are there on a Multilith machine model 1200?

5. What do you call the rollers which take the paper from the feeder foot?

6. What do you call the image produced photographically by exposing through a screen?

7. What is the usual reason for double impressions?

8. How many cylinders are there on a Multilith machine?

9. What do you call the printing process in which the plate itself does not touch the paper?

10. What is wrong with the machine when sheets catch up with one another on the conveyor?

# KEY (CORRECT ANSWERS)

1. Feed (feeder)

2. Varnish
   Reducer

3. Strippers (strips) (straps)
   Tapes
   Bands

4. 4

5. Pull-out (feed) (feeder) (pull-in) (ejector)

6. Half tone

7. Loose blanket
   Too much pressure (pressure not adjusted)

8. 3

9. Offset
   Lithograph
   Planograph

10. Out of time (timing)
    Belt loose

# TEST 2

DIRECTIONS: Directly and concisely, using brief answer form, answer the
following questions.

1. What do you mean by a form "walking off" the plate?

2. What do you use to remove an "image spot" from the plate?

3. What causes the "feeder foot" to grip the paper?

4. Why do you tear rather than cut the edges of the paper used in making underlays?

5. What is the FIRST thing you wash a plate with that has been stored?

6. What is the FIRST liquid you apply after "running" a plate?

7. When plate pressure across the blanket is correct, how wide is the surface
   contacted?

8. What cloth is used as a covering for the repellent rollers?

9. What do you call the image produced on the back of a sheet by wet ink on the
   sheet below?

10. What may one use to "touch-up" negatives?

KEY (CORRECT ANSWERS)

1. Image disappearing (getting weak) (going blind) (fading) (getting light)

2. Hone (scotch hone)
   Eraser
   Stone (pumice stone)
   Snake slip
   Retouch stick

3. Suction (air) (vacuum)

4. To prevent sharp edges (to prevent a sharp break)
   Feather edge (taper)
   To prevent ridges (to lay smooth)
   To prevent cutting blanket

5. Water

6. Gum
   Keepeze
   Plate etch (platex) (etch)
   Repellent (repellinx)
   Water

7. 1/8" to 1/4"

8. Molletin
   Flannel
   Linen
   Muslin

9. Offset

10. Opaque (blackout) (pencil)
    Scratching (etching) tool (sharp tool)
    Needle
    Knife

# KEY (CORRECT ANSWERS)

1. Image disappearing (getting weak) (going blind) (fading) (getting light)

2. Hone (scotch hone)
   Eraser
   Stone (pumice stone)
   Snake slip
   Retouch stick

3. Suction (air) (vacuum)

4. To prevent sharp edges (to prevent a sharp break)
   Feather edge (taper)
   To prevent ridges (to lay smooth)
   To prevent cutting blanket

5. Water

6. Gum
   Keepeze
   Plate etch (platex) (etch)
   Repellent (repellinx)
   Water

7. 1/8" to 1/4"

8. Molletin
   Flannel
   Linen
   Muslin

9. Offset

10. Opaque (blackout) (pencil)
    Scratching (etching) tool (sharp tool)
    Needle
    Knife

# TEST 3

DIRECTIONS: Directly and concisely, using brief answer form, answer the following questions.

1. What do you call the small clip on the feeder which holds down the leading edge of the paper?

2. How far up on the sheet should the "grippers" go?

3. What are two metals commonly used to make Multilith plates?

4. On how many sides can the paper "bleed-off"?

5. What chemical process takes place if you store a zinc plate without coating it?

6. What do you call the cylinder which presses the paper against the blanket?

7. On what part of the Multilith machine is the image reversed?

8. How many ejector rollers are there on a Multilith machine?

9. What is the name for the lightest weight paper that can be run on the Multilith machine?

10. One motor of this machine runs the rollers and belts; what does the other motor do?

11. What is the LAST thing you swab a plate with before running it?

———

## KEY (CORRECT ANSWERS)

1. Cat whisker (whisker)
   Duck tongue (tongue)

2. 1/4"
   5/16"
   3/8"

3. Zinc
   Aluminum

4. Three

5. Oxidizes (oxidation) (oxidization)
   Corrodes

6. Platen
   Impression (impression cylinder)

7. Blanket

8. 2
   4

9. Onionskin
   Nine pound (No. 9)
   Tissue
   Manifold
   Thirteen pound (No. 13)

10. Runs pump (runs suction)(runs compressor)(runs blower)(runs vacuum)
        (runs air pump)
    Runs feeder

11. Platex (etch) (plate etch)

# ABSTRACT REASONING

## SPATIAL PERCEPTION

The spatial relations test, including that phase designated as
atial perception, involves and measures the ability to solve problems,
awn up in the form of outlines or pictures, which are concerned with
e shapes of objects or the interrelationship of their parts.  While,
ncededly, little is known about the nature and scope of this aptitude,
 appears that this ability is required in science, mathematics, engin-
ring, and drawing courses and curricula.  Accordingly, tests of spatial
rception involving the reconstruction of two and three dimensional pat-
rns, are presented in this section.

It is to be noted that the relationships expressed in spatial tests
e geometric, definitive, and exact.  Keeping these basic characteris-
cs in mind, the applicant is to proceed to solve the spatial perception
oblems in his own way.  There is no set method of solving these problems.
e examinee may find that there are different methods for different types
 spatial problems.  Therefore, the BEST way to prepare for this type of
st is to *TAKE* and study the work-practice problems in two and three di-
ntional patterns provided in this section.

———

# SPATIAL RELATIONS - TWO DIMENSIONS

The tests of spatial relations that follow consist of items which involve the visualization of two dimensions.

Each of the items of these tests consists of a line of figures -- a complete figure on the left and four lettered alternatives of component parts on the right, only one of which can be fitted together exactly to form the complete figure on the left.

The candidate is then required to select that choice of component parts which could be fitted together to form the complete figure given at the left.

---

## SAMPLE QUESTIONS AND EXPLANATIONS

DIRECTIONS: The items in this part constitute a test of spatial relations involving two dimensions. Each item consists of a line of figures. The first figure is the complete figure. This is followed by four lettered choices of component parts, only one of which can be fitted together exactly to form the first (complete) figure.

Rules to be followed:
1. The lettered choice of component parts selected as the answer must have the same number of parts as the first (complete) figure.
2. The parts must fit exactly.
3. The parts may be turned around but may not be turned over.

1.
 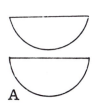   

The correct answer is D. When the two parts of D are completely closed, they form the complete figure on the left.

2.

The correct answer is B. When the two parts of B are reversed in position, they form the complete figure on the left.

1

# TYPE 1

## TEST 1

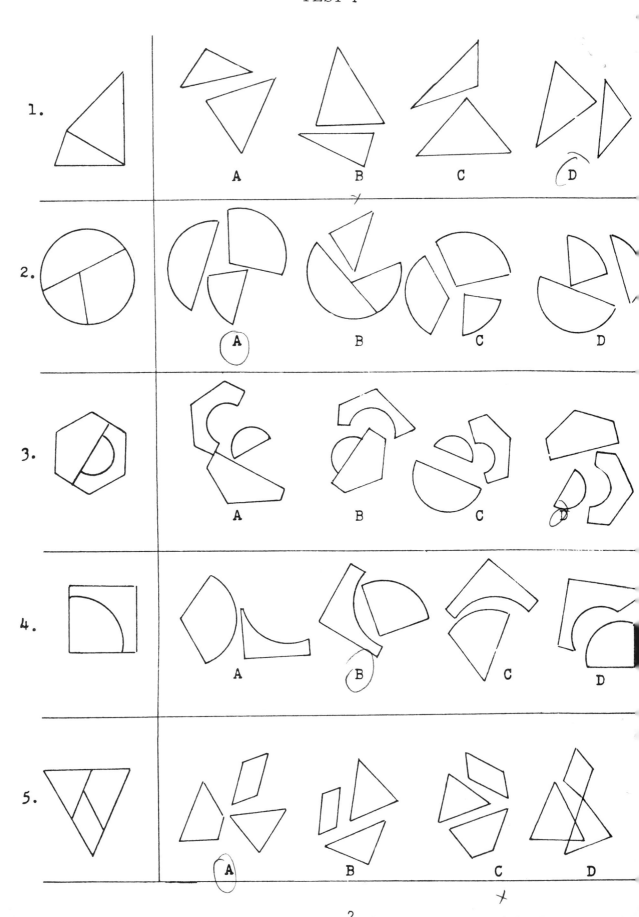

1.
    A    B    C    D

2.
    A    B    C    D

3.
    A    B    C    D

4.
    A    B    C    D

5.
    A    B    C    D

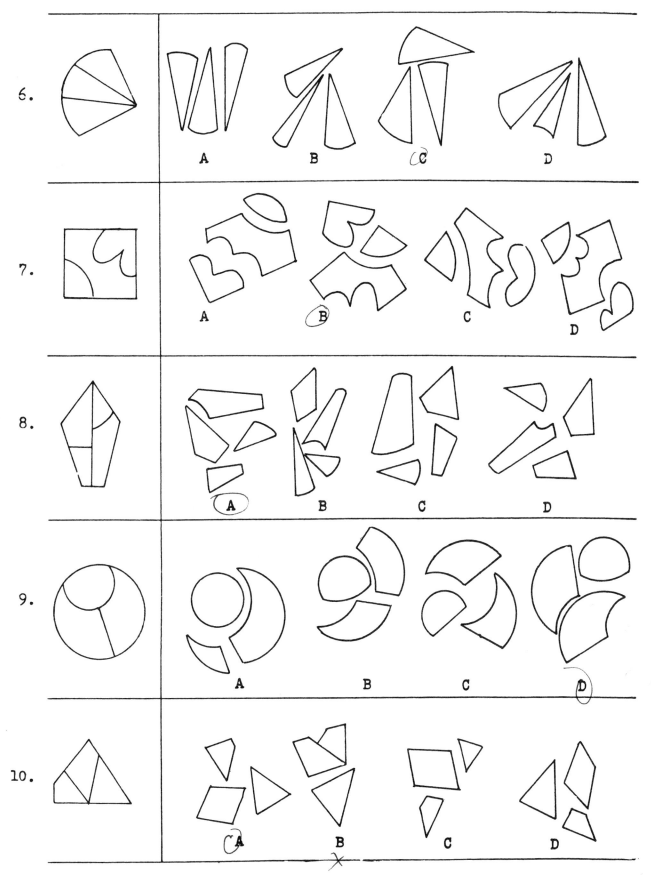

6.

A     B     C     D

7.

A     B     C     D

8.

A     B     C     D

9.

A     B     C     D

10.

A     B     C     D

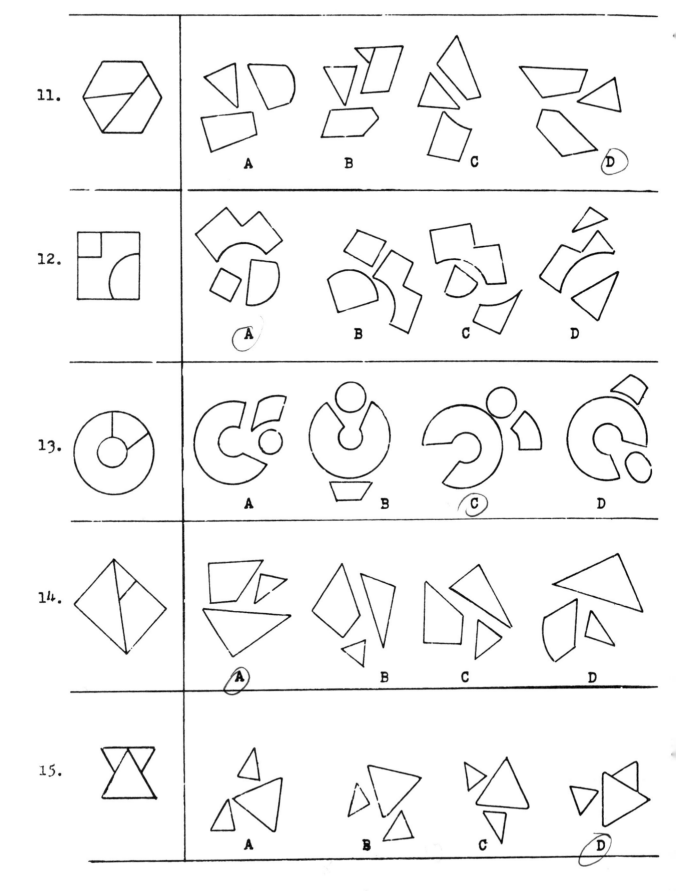

11. A B C D

12. A B C D

13. A B C D

14. A B C D

15. A B C D

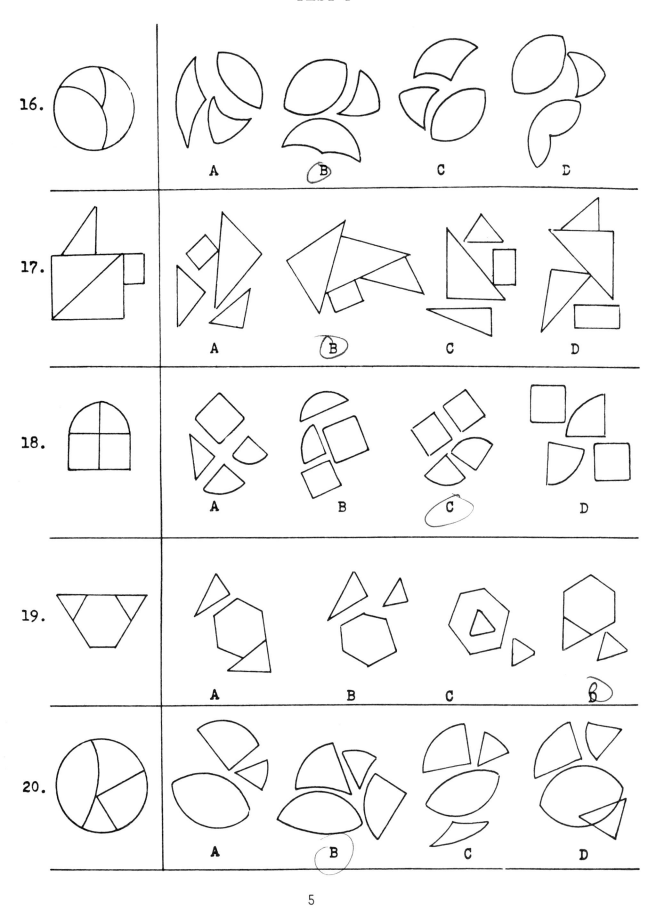

16.

A    B    C    D

17.

A    B    C    D

18.

A    B    C    D

19.

A    B    C    D

20.

A    B    C    D

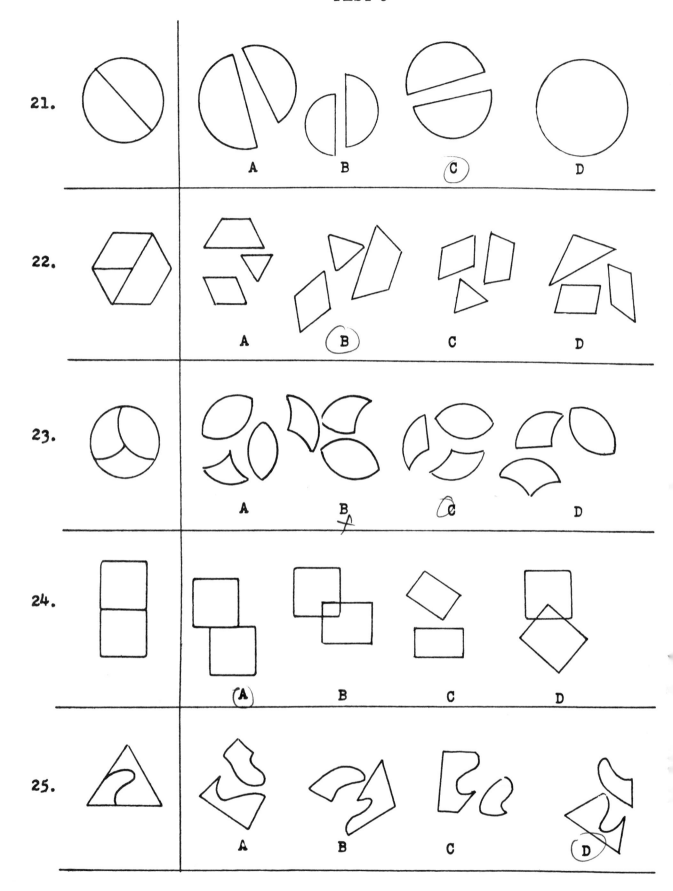

21.  A    B    C    D

22.  A    B    C    D

23.  A    B    C    D

24.  (A)    B    C    D

25.  A    B    C    D

# TYPE 2

DIRECTIONS: Tests 1-7.
   Each of the items in these Tests numbered 1 to 52 is followed by a group of five (5) figures lettered A, B, C, D, and E. Two of these lettered figures, when put together, make the drawing that appears unlettered in the upper left corner. Write on the answer sheet the letters of the two figures which, when put together, are *MOST NEARLY* the same as the unlettered figure.

## TEST 1

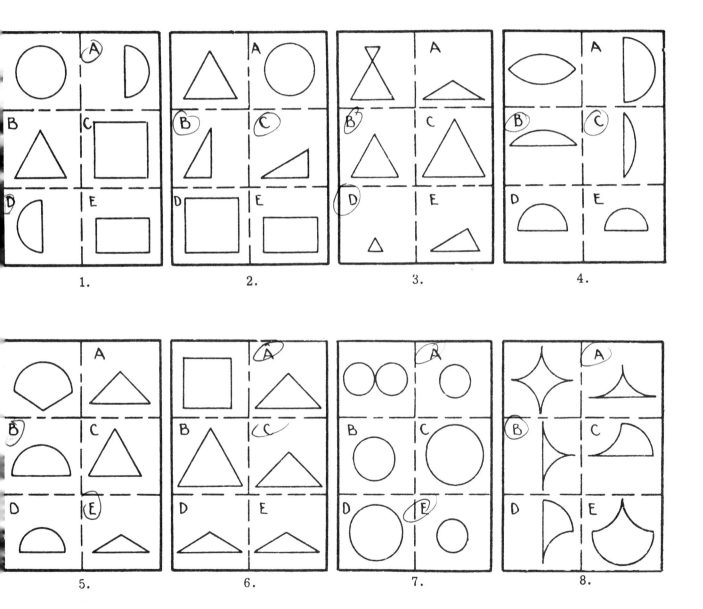

1.        2.        3.        4.

5.        6.        7.        8.

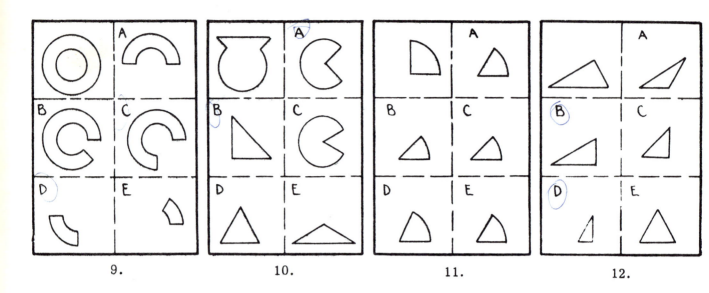

9.    10.    11.    12.

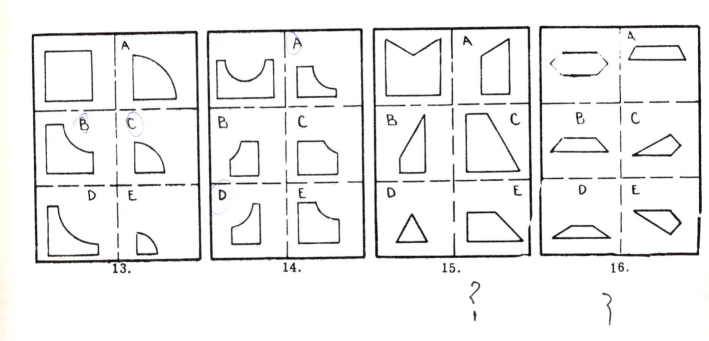

13.    14.    15.    16.

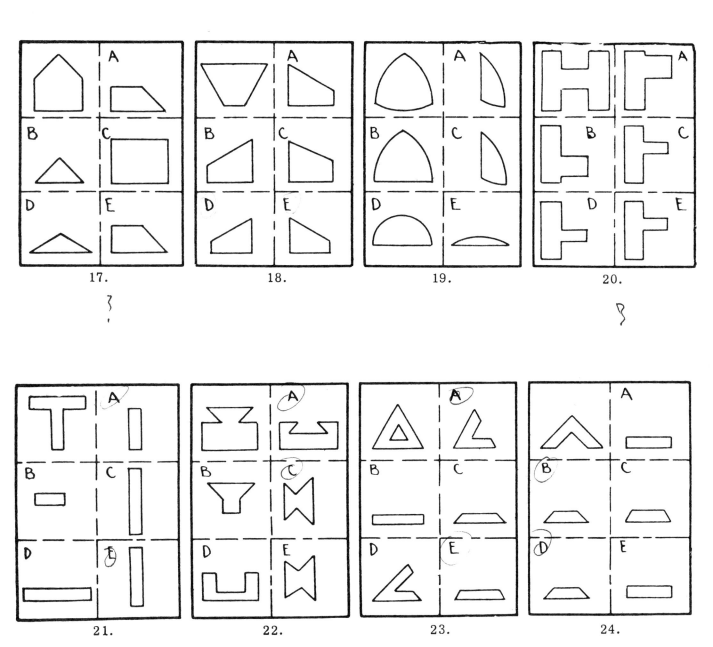

17.

18.

19.

20.

21.

22.

23.

24.

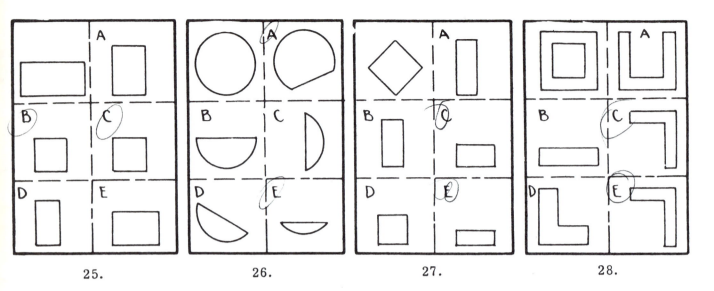

25.      26.      27.      28.

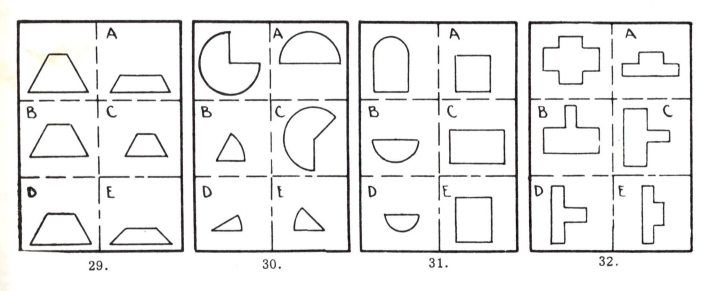

29.      30.      31.      32.

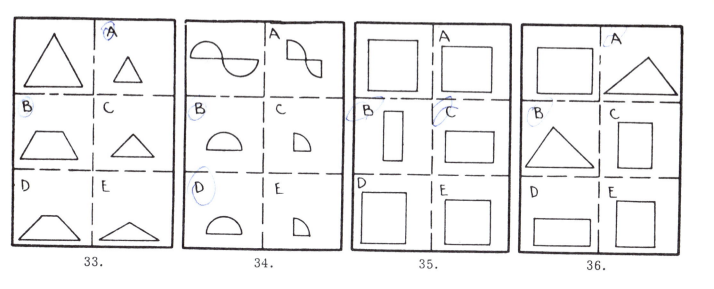

33.   34.   35.   36.

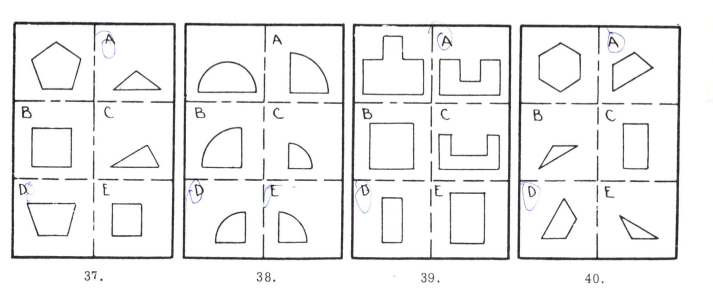

37.   38.   39.   40.

41.  42.  43.  44.

45.  46.  47.  48.

TEST 7

49.  50.  51.  52.

# KEY : CORRECT ANSWERS

## SPATIAL RELATIONS - TWO DIMENSIONS

### TYPE 1 - TESTS 1 - 5

| TEST 1 | | TEST 2 | | TEST 3 | | TEST 4 | | TEST 5 | |
|---|---|---|---|---|---|---|---|---|---|
| 1. | B | 6. | C | 11. | D | 16. | B | 21. | C |
| 2. | A | 7. | B | 12. | A | 17. | B | 22. | B |
| 3. | D | 8. | A | 13. | C | 18. | C | 23. | B |
| 4. | B | 9. | D | 14. | A | 19. | D | 24. | A |
| 5. | C | 10. | B | 15. | D | 20. | B | 25. | D |

---

### TYPE 2 - TESTS 1 - 7

| TEST 1 | | TEST 2 | | TEST 3 | | TEST 4 | | TEST 5 | |
|---|---|---|---|---|---|---|---|---|---|
| 1. | AD | 9. | CD | 17. | AE | 25. | BC | 33. | AB |
| 2. | BC | 10. | AB | 18. | DE | 26. | AE | 34. | BD |
| 3. | BD | 11. | BC | 19. | BE | 27. | CE | 35. | BC |
| 4. | BD | 12. | BD | 20. | CD or | 28. | CE | 36. | AB |
| 5. | BE | 13. | BC | | DE or | 29. | AC | 37. | AD |
| 6. | AC | 14. | AD | | CE | 30. | CE | 38. | DE |
| 7. | AE | 15. | CD | 21. | AE | 31. | AD | 39. | AD |
| 8. | AB | 16. | CE | 22. | AC | 32. | AE | 40. | AD |
| | | | | 23. | AE | | | | |
| | | | | 24. | BD | | | | |

| TEST 6 | | TEST 7 | |
|---|---|---|---|
| 41. | CD | 49. | BE |
| 42. | CD | 50. | CE |
| 43. | CE | 51. | BE |
| 44. | CD | 52. | AE |
| 45. | AD | | |
| 46. | AD | | |
| 47. | CD | | |
| 48. | DE | | |

# SPATIAL RELATIONS - THREE DIMENSIONS

The tests of spatial relations that follow consist of items which involve the visualization of three dimensions.

Each of the items of these tests consists of a line of figures -- a question figure in stretchout or open form on the left and five lettered figures on the right, one of which will most closely represent the stretchout or open figure when the latter is folded together.

The candidate is then required to select the figure which will most closely represent the stretchout or open figure when the latter is folded together.

––––––

## SAMPLE QUESTIONS AND EXPLANATIONS

DIRECTIONS: The items in this part constitute a test of spatial relations involving three dimensions. Each item consists of a line of figures. The first figure is the question figure which appears in stretchout or open form. This is followed by five lettered figures which appear in three-dimensional form. When the stretchout or open figure is folded together, which of the five figures will it most closely represent?

Rules to be followed:
1. The stretchout figure may be folded along the lines or rolled where necessary.
2. The edges of the stretchout figure must meet exactly, with no overlapping or empty spaces between them.

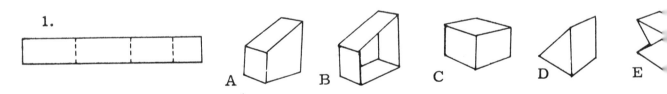

The correct answer is B. This is a simple fold of a four-sided figure.

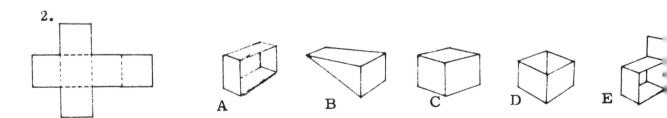

The correct answer is C. This represents the product of a continuous fold from any point to form a cube (six-sided solid).

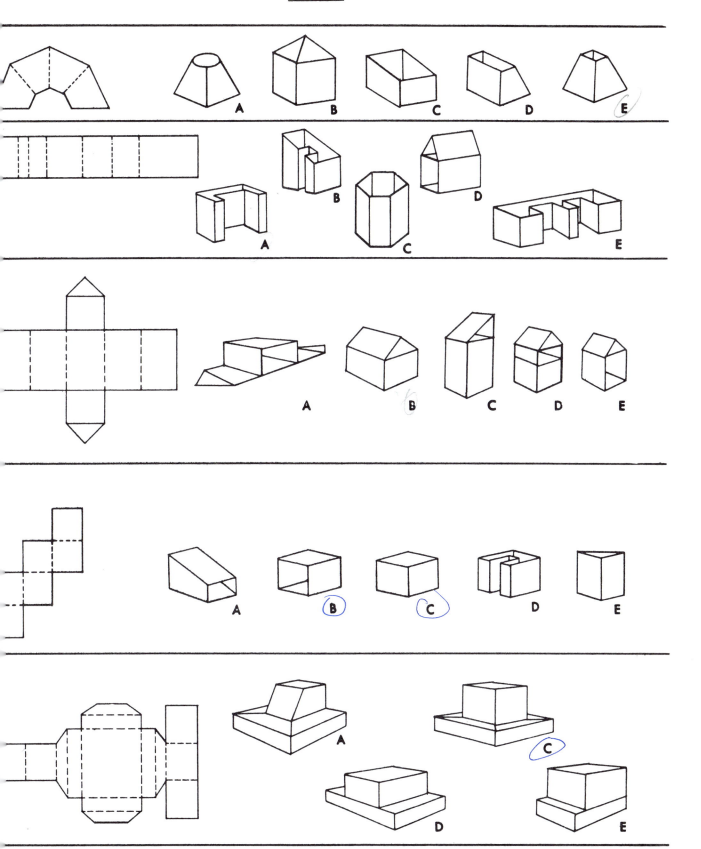

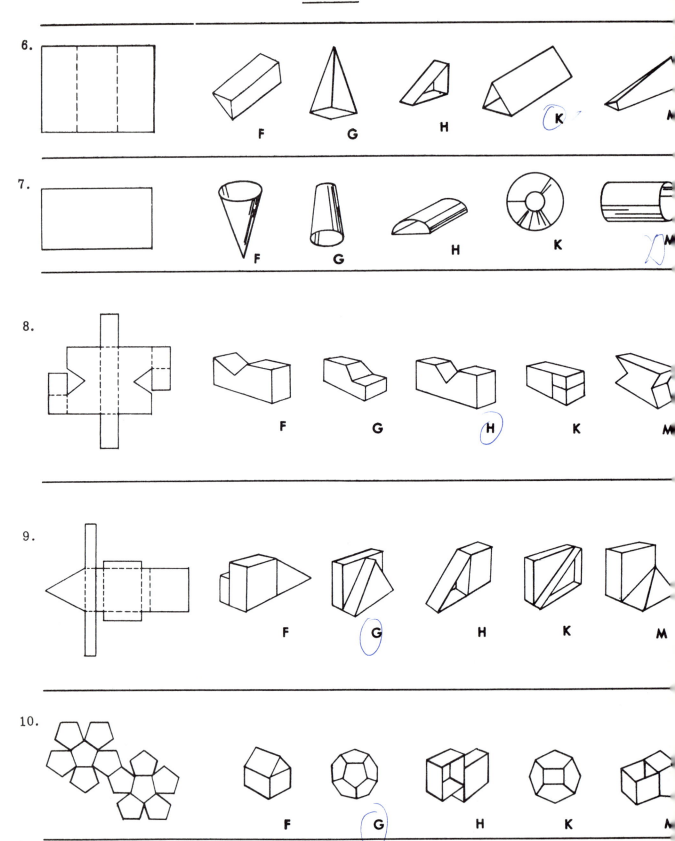

6.  F G H K M

7.  F G H K M

8.  F G H K M

9.  F G H K M

10. F G H K M

11.

2.

.

4.

5.

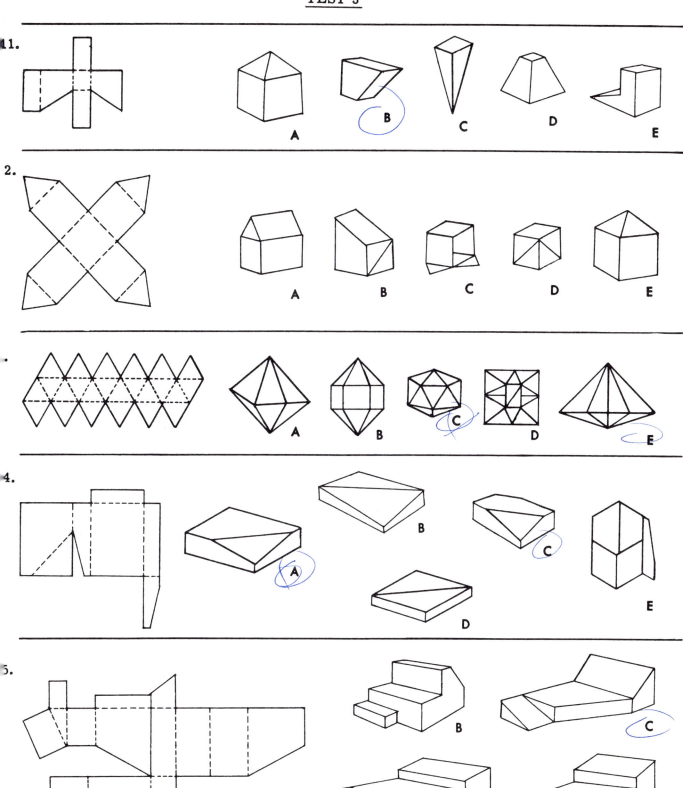

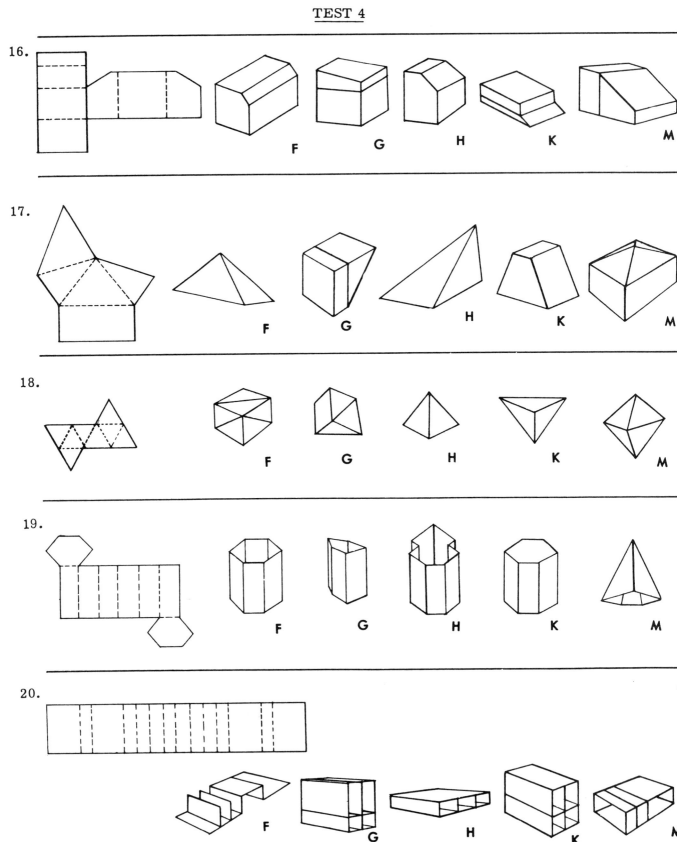

16.

F    G    H    K    M

17.

F    G    H    K    M

18.

F    G    H    K    M

19.

F    G    H    K    M

20.

F    G    H    K    M

# KEYS : CORRECT ANSWERS

## SPATIAL RELATIONS - THREE DIMENSIONS

TEST 1      Explanation
1. E      Straight edges form square-top hollow pyramid
2. A      Count panels for key
3. B      Solid "house" shape
4. C      Solid cube shape
5. C      Fold all sides toward center

TEST 2
6. K      Simple three panel fold
7. M      Roll left to right
8. H      Fold all sides toward the center
9. G      Fold all sides toward the center
10. G     A continuous fold from any point to form a dodecahedron
          (based on a single pentagon form)

TEST 3
11. B     Fold toward the center
12. E     Cube with pyramid on top
13. C     Continuous fold to form an icositetrahedron (24 planes);
          based on equilateral triangles
14. A     Size of triangular fold is the key
15. C     Fold all sides toward the center

TEST 4
16. H     Fold from left to right
17. F     Pyramid with base
18. M     Continuous fold to form an octahedron, based on two pyramids,
          bottom to bottom
19. K     Hexagon (solid)
20. G     Count panels and start fold from the center, working both sides
          together

# PATTERN ANALYSIS (RIGHT SIDE ELEVATION)

## Sample Question

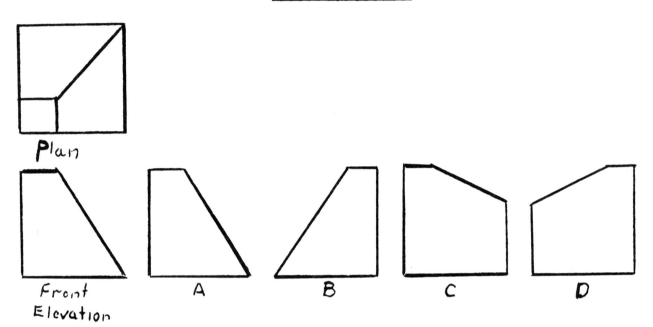

Plan

Front
Elevation

A    B    C    D

In the sample shown above, which figure *CORRECTLY* represents the right side elevation?

    1.  A       2.  B       3.  C       4.  D

The *CORRECT* answer is 1.

## TEST 1

Questions 1-5.

DIRECTIONS:  In questions 1 through 5 which follow, the plan and front elevation of an object are shown on the left, and on the right are shown four figures one of which, and ONLY one, represents the right side elevation. Mark on your answer sheet the number which represents the right side elevation

                 1.  A      2.  B    3.  C    4.  D

1.

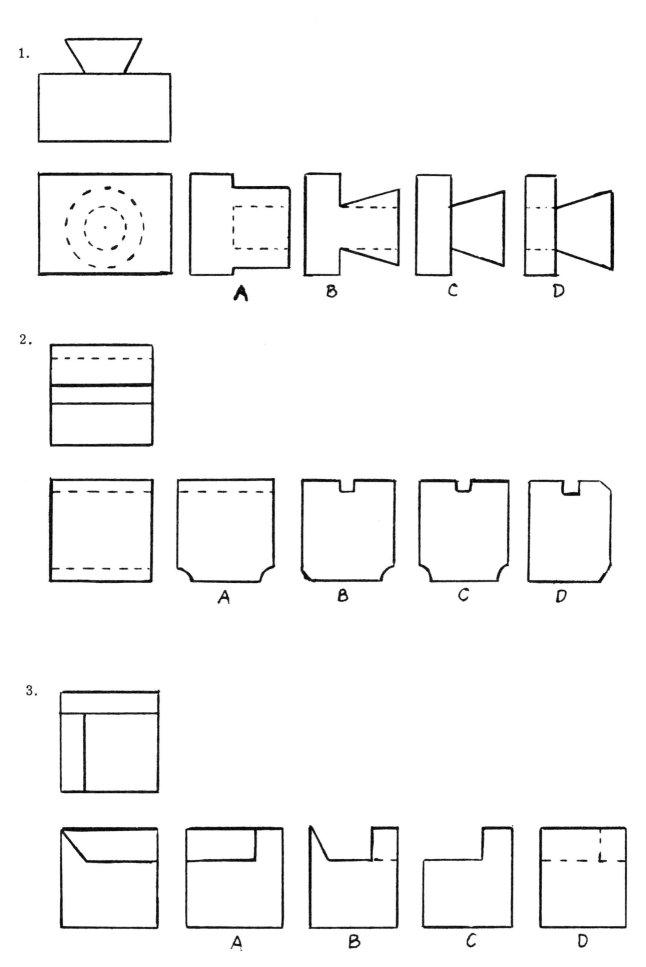

A  B  C  D

2.

A  B  C  D

3.

A  B  C  D

21

4.

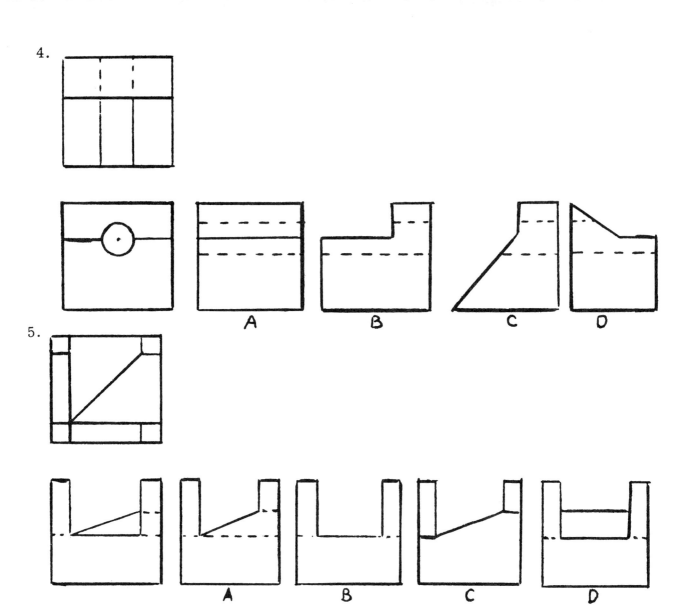

5.

A    B    C    D

A    B    C    D

<u>KEY (CORRECT ANSWERS)</u>

| | |
|---|---|
| 1. | 4 |
| 2. | 3 |
| 3. | 3 |
| 4. | 2 |
| 5. | 2 |

# PATTERN ANALYSIS (END ELEVATION)

Questions 1-5.

DIRECTIONS: In each of the following groups of drawings the top view and
front elevation of an object are shown at the left. At the
right are four drawings, one of which represents the end elevation of the object as seen from the right. Select the drawing which represents the *CORRECT* end elevation.
The first group is shown as a sample ONLY. Which drawing represents the *CORRECT* end elevation? 1. A 2. B 3. C 4. D
The *CORRECT* answer is 3.

<u>Sample Question</u>

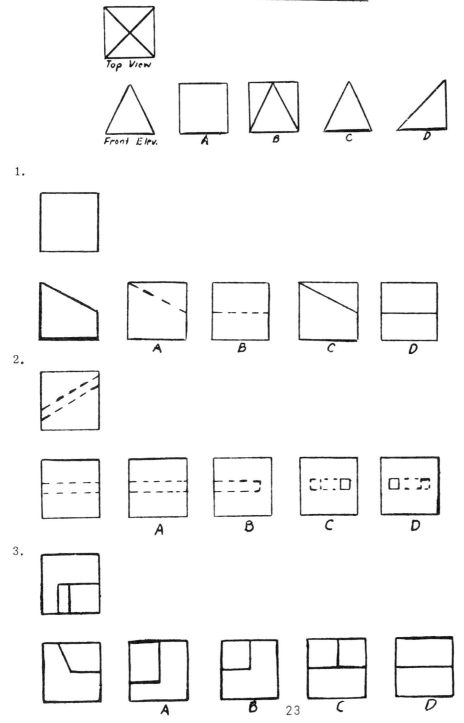

**4.**

 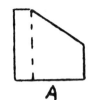 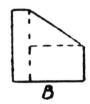 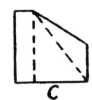 

A      B      C      D

**5.**

  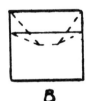  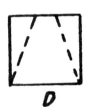

A      B      C      D

## KEY (CORRECT ANSWERS)

| | |
|---|---|
| 1. | 4 |
| 2. | 3 |
| 3. | 2 |
| 4. | 1 |
| 5. | 1 |

# PATTERN ANALYSIS (RIGHT SIDE VIEW)

<u>TEST 1</u>

Questions 1-5.

DIRECTIONS: In each of questions 1 to 5 inclusive, two views of an object
are given. Of the views labelled A, B, C, and D, select the
one that *CORRECTLY* represents the right side view of each object.
Which view represents the right side view? 1. A  2. B  3. C
4. D

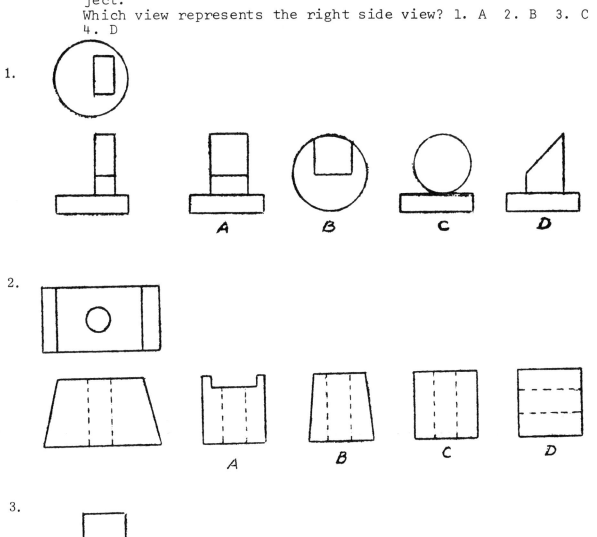

1.

2.

3.

25

4.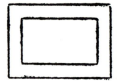

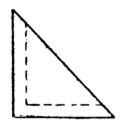 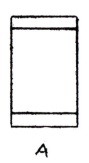 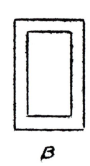 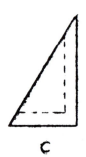 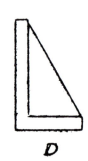

A        B        C        D

5.

 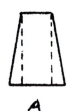 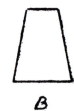  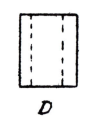

A        B        C        D

## KEY (CORRECT ANSWERS)

|     |   |
|-----|---|
| 1.  | 4 |
| 2.  | 3 |
| 3.  | 3 |
| 4.  | 2 |
| 5.  | 2 |

# BASIC FUNDAMENTALS OF BLUEPRINT READING

## CHAPTER 1

## BLUEPRINTS

A picture is worth a thousand words. Man has used pictures as a means of communication for many years. It would be almost impossible for an engineer or an inventor to describe the size and shape of a simple object without a drawing of some kind. For example, if an engineer designed a simple object such as the oil filter bracket (fig. 1-1) it would be difficult to convey his idea to the person who is to fabricate the object without a drawing to show the shape, size, and location of the holes.

Drawing or sketching is the universal language used by engineers, technicians and skilled craftsmen. Whether this drawing is made freehand or by the use of drawing instruments (mechanical drawing) it is needed to convey all the necessary information to the individual who will fabricate and assemble the object whether it be a building, ship, aircraft, or a mechanical device. If many people are involved in the fabrication of the object, copies will be made of the original drawing or tracing so that all persons involved will have the same information.

Not only are drawings (prints) used as plans to fabricate and assemble objects, they also may be used to illustrate how machines, ships, aircraft, and so on are operated, maintained, repaired or lubricated.

### HOW PRINTS ARE MADE

Blueprints are reproduced copies of mechanical or other types of technical drawings, other than the arts (painting, water coloring, etc.).

A mechanical drawing is drawn with instruments such as compasses, ruling pens, T-squares, triangles, and french curves. Prints are reproduced from original drawings in much the same manner as photographic prints are reproduced from negatives.

The original drawings for prints are made by drawing directly on, or tracing a drawing on a translucent tracing paper or cloth, using black waterproof (india) ink or a special pencil. This original drawing is normally referred to as a tracing (master copy). These copies of the tracings are rarely, if ever, sent to a shop or job site. Instead, reproductions of these tracings are made and distributed to persons or offices where needed. These tracings can be used over and over indefinitely if properly handled and stored.

From these tracings, mentioned in the previous paragraph, blueprints are made. The term blueprint is a rather loosely used term in dealing with reproductions of original drawings. One of the first processes devised to reproduce or duplicate tracings produced white lines on a blue background, hence the term blueprints. Today, however, other methods of reproduction have been developed, and they produce prints of different colors. The colors may be brown, black, gray, or maroon. The differences lie in the types of paper and the developing processes used.

A patented paper identified as "BW" paper produces prints with black lines on a white background.

The ammonia process or "OZALIDS" produces prints with either black, blue, or maroon lines on a white background.

Vandyke paper produces a white line on a dark brown background.

Other processes that may be used to reproduce drawings, usually small drawings or sketches, are the office type duplicating machines such as the Mimeograph, ditto machines, and the like. One other type of duplicating process rarely used for reproducing working drawings is the photostatic process. This in reality is a photographic process in which a large camera reduces or enlarges a tracing or drawing. The photostat has white lines on a dark background when reproduced directly from a tracing or drawing. If the photostated print is then reproduced it will have brown lines on a

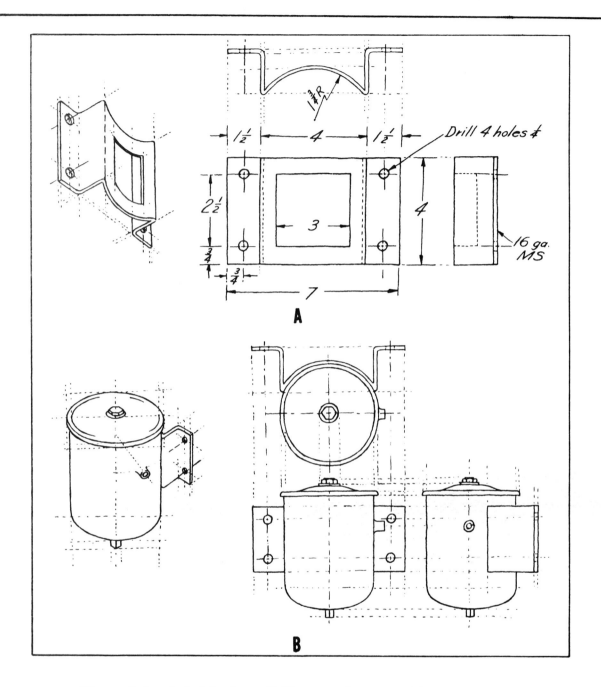

Figure 1-1.—A sketch of an oil filter bracket and oil filter assembly.

white background. Photostats are generally used by various businesses for incorporating reduced size drawings into reports or records.

HANDLING BLUEPRINTS

Blueprints or prints are valuable permanent records that can be used over and over again if

necessary. However, if you are to keep these prints as permanent records, you must handle them with care. Here are a few simple rules to follow to preserve these prints:

1. Keep them out of strong sunlight—they will fade.

2. Don't allow them to get wet or smudged with oil or grease; these ingredients seldom dry

2

out completely, thereby making the prints practically useless.

3. Don't make pencil or crayon notations on a print without proper authority. If you get instructions to mark a print, use an appropriate colored pencil and make the markings a permanent part of the print. Yellow is a good color to use on a print with a blue background (blueprint).

4. Keep prints stowed in their proper place so they can be readily located the next time you want to refer to them.

## FOLDING BLUEPRINTS

A standardized, accurate system of filing blueprints is necessary in order to have them readily available when necessary.

Most of the prints that you will handle will be received properly folded. Your main concern will be to refold them correctly. You may, however, have occasion to receive prints that have not been folded at all, or have been folded improperly.

The method of folding prints depends upon the type and size of the filing cabinet, and the location of the identifying marks on the prints. It is preferable to place identifying marks at the top of prints when filing them vertically (upright), and at the bottom right corner, when filing them flat. In some cases construction prints are stored in rolls.

### TYPES OF DRAWINGS

In subsequent chapters, the various types of projections, schematics, and diagrams used in machine, architectural and structural, electrical, electronics, plumbing or piping, and topographical drawings, will be covered in detail. In this chapter, several popular types of graphs and charts will be explained briefly.

### CHARTS AND GRAPHS

Charts and graphs are primarily used to show organization, for analysis of data, and for presentation of statistics for comparison or prediction. The underlying principle of charts and graphs is to show the subdivisions of a whole and the relationship of its parts to one another.

Figure 1-2 shows the organization of the operating forces of the Navy. In interpreting this chart, it shows that the Chief of Naval Operations is responsible for the command, use and

administration of the operating forces of the Navy. Directly responsible to the Chief or Naval Operations are: The Commander-in-Chief of the Pacific Fleet (CINCPACFLT), the Commander-in-Chief of the Atlantic Fleet (CINCLANTFLT), the Commander-in-Chief, U. S. Naval Forces in Europe (CINCUSNAVEUR), Commander of Military Sea Transportation Service (COMSTS), and the Coast Guard when they are operating as a service in the Navy. The blocks directly shown beneath each of these commanders designate the various commands who are directly responsible to them. For example, the First and Seventh Fleets and the other commands listed in this block are under the direct command of (CINCPACFLT).

Illustrated in figure 1-3 is a simple bar graph, showing the number of personnel by naval districts, who have been instructed in character training by chaplains. You will note in this graph, that the exact figures are given at the end of each bar; normally these figures are not given. When the figures are not given at the end of each bar you would normally round out the figures. For example, in this graph you would probably read the bar designating PRNC to be 97, 500 or 98, 000.

The graph shown in figure 1-4 is known as a line graph. The line graph is generally used to show increases or decreases in money, material, personnel, and so on, usually over a definite time period.

In reading the line graph in figure 1-4 (DISTRICT), marked in the heavy black line, you can see that 546,976 persons were instructed up to 31 December 1953. There was a drop of approximately 16,000 in the first part of 1954, then a tremendous increase of approximately 400,000, in the second part of 1954; finally, there was a slight decline of approximately 19,000 to June of 1955.

Another popular type of chart or diagram is the PIE chart. The pie chart represents a 100 percent circle. Figure 1-5 indicates the percentage and types of elements that are used to meet the standard specification of ASTM (American Society for Testing Materials) B-21, a naval specification for brass bars, rods and shapes. The pie chart shows that the B-21 metal is made of the following elements: zinc, 36.6 percent; copper, 62 percent; tin, 1 percent; lead, .20 percent maximum; iron, .10 percent maximum; other elements, .10 percent maximum. Adding up all the elements shown in the pie chart will give you a total of 100 percent.

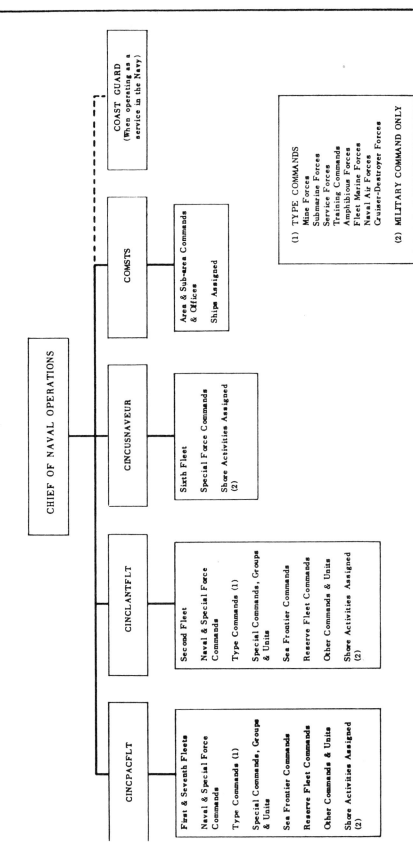

Figure 1-2.—Organization chart.

4

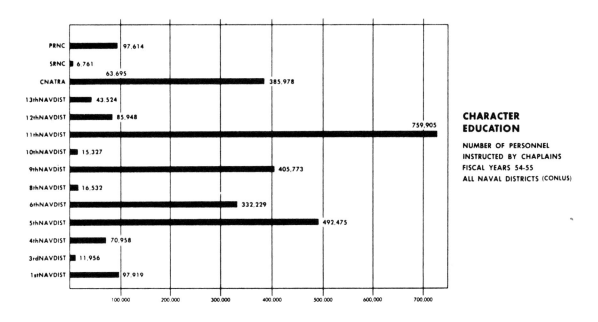

Figure 1-3.—Bar graph.

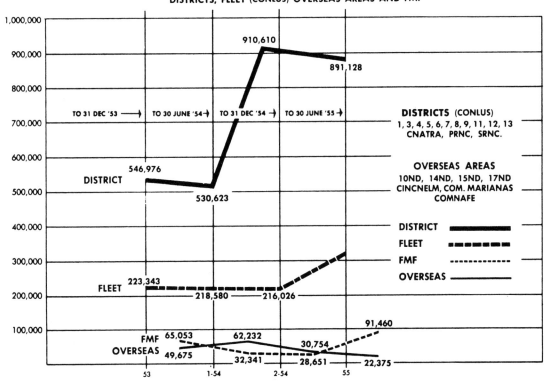

Figure 1-4.—Line graph.

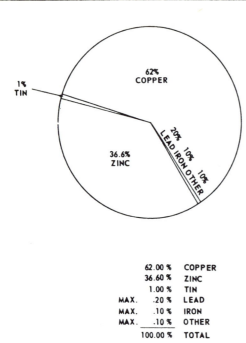

| | | |
|---|---:|---|
| | 62.00 % | COPPER |
| | 36.60 % | ZINC |
| | 1.00 % | TIN |
| MAX. | .20 % | LEAD |
| MAX. | .10 % | IRON |
| MAX. | .10 % | OTHER |
| | 100.00 % | TOTAL |

Figure 1-5.—Pie chart.

## CRITICAL PATH METHOD DIAGRAM

Another type of graph now in prominent use is the critical path planning method diagram. The critical path method is an outgrowth of the Program Evaluation Review Technique (PERT) developed in the Special Projects Office of the Bureau of Naval Weapons.

This manual will give you a brief explanation of a simple critical path diagram for constructing a building foundation (footing) (figure 1-6).

The critical path is defined as the longest line or path through DEPENDENT SEQUENCES of activities from start to finish. In figure 1-6, you will note that the critical path is the heavy line preceded by a node and terminated by an arrow (3 are shown). The dependent sequences in this case are: excavating, erecting and building forms, and pouring and finishing the concrete. The forms cannot be built and erected until the excavation is completed; the concrete cannot be poured until the forms and reinforcing bars are in place.

In reading the diagram in figure 1-6, beginning with node "o", the first phase of the critical path is the excavating. You will note on the

diagram that the excavating will be completed in 1 1/2 days (8-hour days). The diagram shows further that, during the period of excavation, the soil pipe, reinforcing bars (rebars), and the lumber can be picked up and delivered to the site in approximately 7 hours; this is shown by the noncritical path lines preceded by nodes 1, 2, and 3. The noncritical path lines are shown on the diagram as being thinner than the critical path line. The dashes (----) at the end of the noncritical path lines indicate float time (free time). In reading this diagram, float time would be approximately 5 hours prior to the completion of the first stage of critical path activity. A critical path line will never indicate float time. The noncritical path activities can be defined as those activities that can be accomplished while another more critical activity is being accomplished.

Node 4 is the beginning of the second sequence of the critical path, and nodes 5 and 6 are the noncritical path of the second sequence, which indicate that while the forms are being built the soil pipe can be placed and back filled, and the rebars can be placed and tied. The diagram further indicates that noncritical paths 5 and 6 have approximately 2 hours of float time. The third and final sequence along the critical path, (node 7) is the pouring and finishing of the concrete footing; the diagram indicates that the project will be completed at the end of the third day. Note that the critical and noncritical sequence (cleanup) are to be completed at the same time, no float time being shown on the noncritical path.

## WORKING DRAWINGS

A working drawing is any drawing which is complete enough to give the craftsman all the information needed to fabricate an object. The object referred to may be a bearing for a machine, it may be an aircraft, or a building. A simple object such as the "guide pin" (figure 1-7) will require only two views and have all the necessary information on the print. The oil filter bracket, shown earlier in figure 1-1 required 3 views including an assembly sketch to show the completed object and the position of the parts.

In architectural prints, a full set of views is furnished to give the craftsmen all the information required to construct the building. Figure 1-8 shows all views necessary for the craftsmen

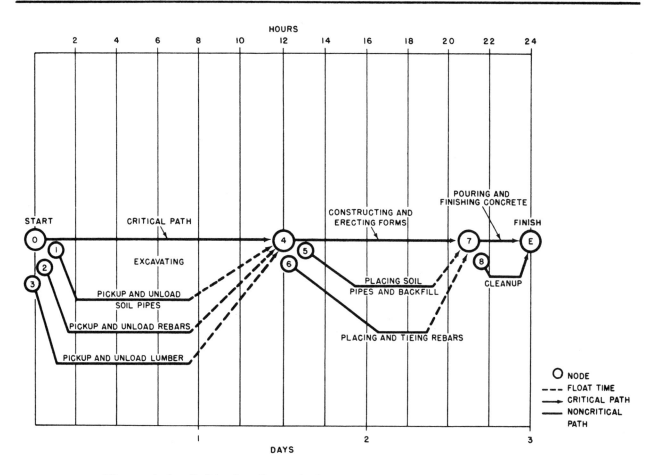

Figure 1-6.—Critical path method diagram for constructing a footing.

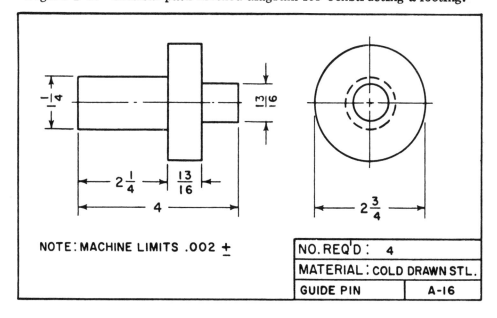

NOTE: MACHINE LIMITS .002 ±

| NO. REQ'D : | 4 |
|---|---|
| MATERIAL : COLD DRAWN STL. | |
| GUIDE PIN | A-16 |

Figure 1-7.—A simple working drawing (machine).

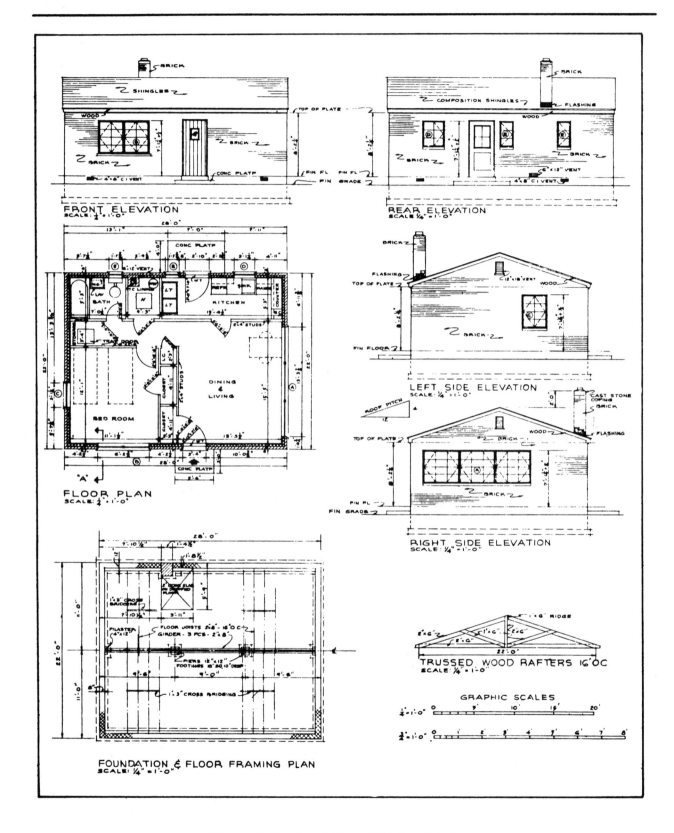

Figure 1-8.—A set of architectural prints.

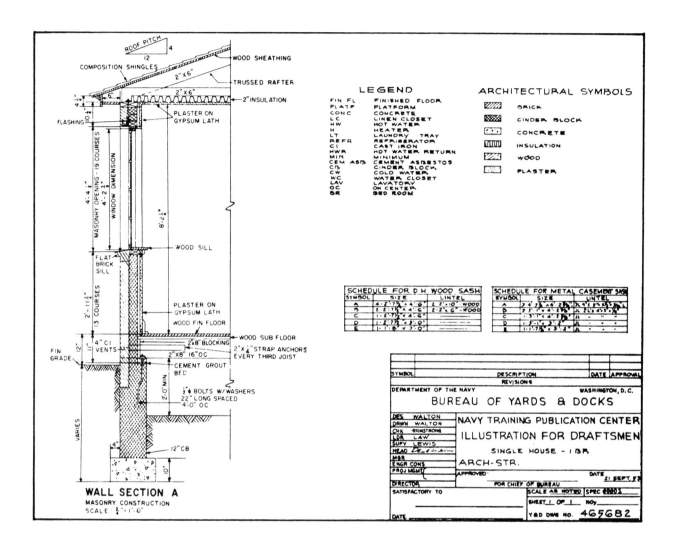

Figure 1-8.—A set of architectural prints—continued.

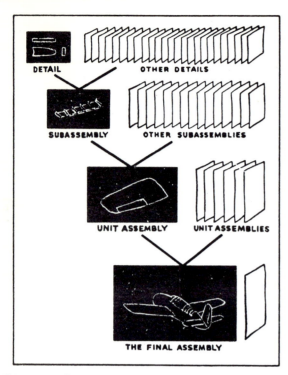

DETAIL    OTHER DETAILS

SUBASSEMBLY    OTHER SUBASSEMBLIES

UNIT ASSEMBLY    UNIT ASSEMBLIES

THE FINAL ASSEMBLY

Figure 1-9.—Every part, every assembly has its descriptive print.

to build the building, including a detail of the cornice and the foundation.

Figure 1-9 shows the types of working drawings required to construct an aircraft. The assembling of an aircraft, in this case begins with a detail print of the aileron rib; the figure also indicates that the set of prints may contain other details. Then there is a subassembly print that shows how the aileron rib joins the other parts of the aileron assembly. Next is a unit assembly print, which shows you where the aileron joins the other parts of the wing assembly. The final assembly print shows the entire wing assembly in relation to the completed aircraft.

# CHAPTER 2

# PARTS OF A BLUEPRINT

The name of the object on the blueprint is given in the title block (figs. 2-1 and 2-2), which is located in the lower right corner of all drawings prepared according to Military Standards (MIL-STD-2B, 25 Aug. 1960). Figure 2-1 is the type of title block used in Yards and Docks construction drawings. Figure 2-2 is the type used by BuShips for technical drawings. The title block may appear elsewhere on other blueprints, but the lower right corner is the usual place.

## TITLE BLOCK

The title block contains the drawing number and all the information required to identify the part or assembly that the blueprint represents. In approved military blueprints, the title block will include the name and address of the Government agency or organization preparing the drawing, the scale, drafting record, authentication, and the date.

If a space within the title block has a diagonal or slant line drawn across it, disregard that space, because the diagonal line indicates that the information usually placed in it is not required, or is given elsewhere on the drawing.

## REVISION BLOCK

Each drawing shows a revision block located on the right side of the print. Modern practice

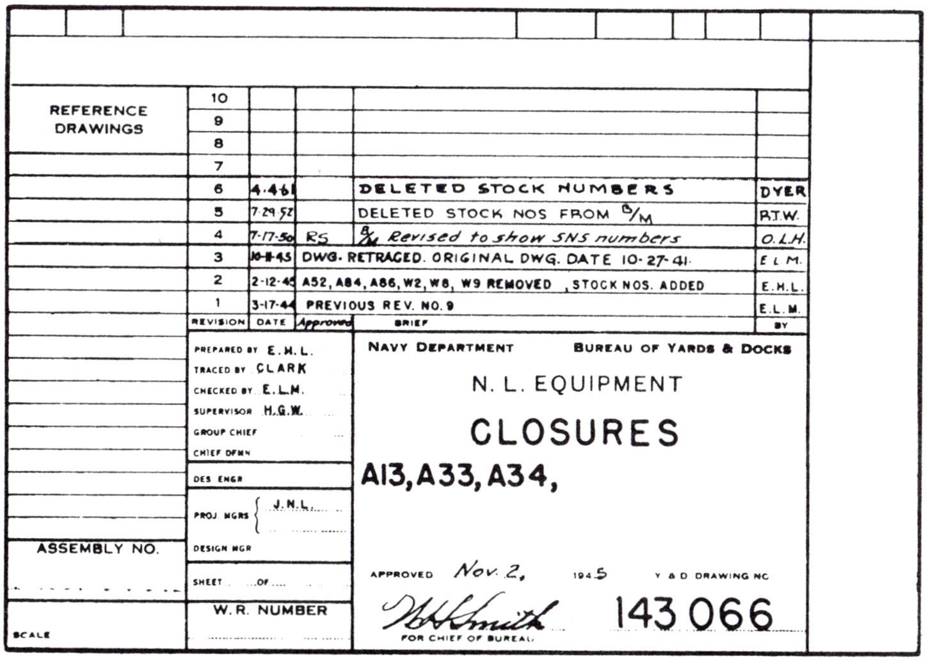

Figure 2-1.—Title block (Yds&Dks).

11

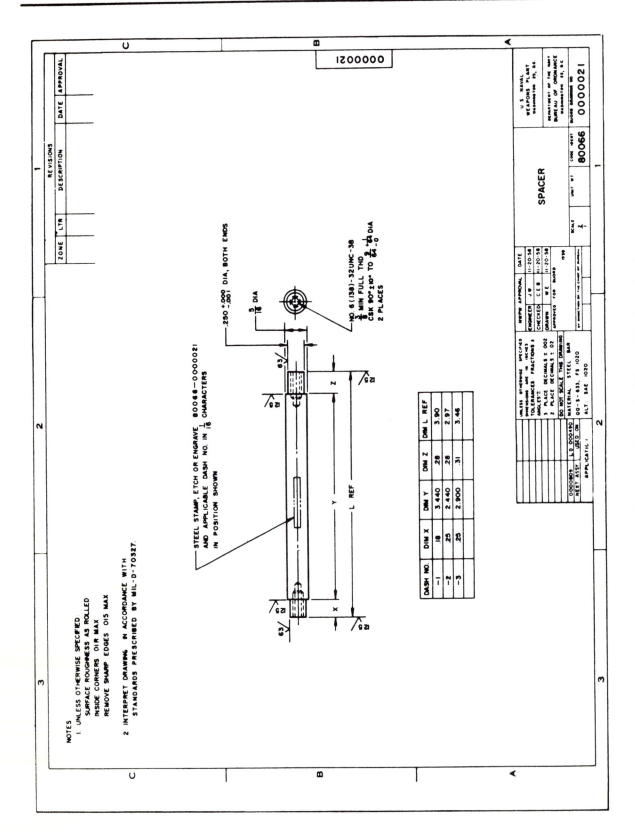

Figure 2-2.—Format of a BuWeps drawing sheet.

is to put this space for the recording of changes in the upper right corner, but it may appear above the title. All changes to the drawing are noted in this block and are dated and identified by a number or a letter. If, for some reason, a revision block is not used, a revised drawing may be shown by the addition of a letter to the original number; for example, if the print shown in figure 2-1 were revised, it would appear as number 143066-A.

DRAWING NUMBER

All drawings are identified by a drawing number, which appears in a number block in the lower right corner of the title block. It may be shown in other places also; for example, near the top border line, in the upper corner, or on the reverse side at both ends so that it will be visible when a drawing is rolled up. Its purpose is to permit quick identification of a blueprint number. If a blueprint has more than one sheet, and each sheet has the same number, this information is included in the number block indicating the sheet number and the number of sheets in the series. For example, note that in the title block shown in figure 2-1, the sheet is page 2 of 8 sheets.

REFERENCE NUMBERS AND
DASH NUMBERS

Reference numbers that appear in the title block refer to numbers of other blueprints. When more than one detail is shown on a drawing, dash and numbers are frequently used. For example, if two parts are shown in one detail drawing. Both prints would have the same drawing number, plus a dash and an individual number, such as, 8117041-1 and 8117041-2.

In addition to appearing in the title block, the dash and numbers may appear on the face of the drawings near the parts they identify. Some commercial prints show the drawing and dash numbers and point with a leader line to the part; others use a circle, 3/8 inch in diameter around the dash number, and carry a leader line to the part.

A dash and numbers are used to identify modified or improved parts, and also to identify right-hand and left-hand parts.

Many aircraft parts on the left-hand side of an aircraft are exactly like the corresponding parts on the right-hand side—in reverse. The left-hand part is always shown in the drawing.

The right-hand part is called for in the title block.

Above the title block you will see a notation, such as "159674 LH shown; 159674-1 RH opposite." Both parts carry the same number. But the part called for is distinguished by a dash and number. LH means left-hand, and RH means right-hand. Some companies use odd numbers for right-hand parts and even numbers for left-hand parts.

ZONE NUMBERS

Zone numbers on blueprints serve the same purpose as the numbers and letters printed on borders of maps to help you locate a particular point. To find a point, you mentally draw horizontal and vertical lines from these letters and numerals, and the point where these lines intersect is the area sought.

You will use practically the same system to help you locate parts, sections, and views on large blueprinted objects (for example, assembly drawings of aircraft). Parts numbered in the title block can be located on the drawing by looking up the numbers in squares along the lower border. Zone numbers read from right to left.

SCALE

The scale of the blueprint is indicated in one of the spaces within the title block. It indicates the size of the drawing as compared with the actual size of the part. The scale is usually shown as 1" = 2", 1" = 12", 1/2" = 1", and so on. It may also be indicated as full size, one-half size, one-fourth size, and so on.

If a blueprint indicates that the scale is 1" = 2", each line on the print is shown one-half its actual length. A scale showing 3" = 1" each line on the print is three times its actual length.

Very small parts are enlarged to show the views clearly, and large objects are normally reduced in size to fit on a standard size drawing paper. In short, the scale is selected to fit the object being drawn and space available on a sheet of drawing paper.

Remember: NEVER MEASURE A DRAWING. USE DIMENSIONS. Why? Because the print may have been reduced in size from the original drawing; reduction errors may have been introduced which you would include by a physical measurement. Or, you might not take the scale of the drawing into consideration. Then, too, paper stretches and shrinks as the humidity changes, thus introducing perhaps, the greatest source of error in actually taking a measurement by laying a rule on the print itself. Play it safe and READ the dimensions on the drawing; they always remain the same.

Graphical scales are often placed on maps and plot plans. These scales indicate the number of feet or miles represented by an inch. A fraction is often used, as 1/500, meaning that one unit on the map is equal to 500 like units on the ground. A LARGE-SCALE MAP has a scale of 1" = 10'; a map with a scale of 1" = 1000' is considered to be a SMALL-SCALE MAP.

### STATION NUMBERS

On large assemblies—aircrafts, for example—a numbering system is used to help locate STATIONS on the aircraft assembly, such as the fuselage frame shown in figure 2-3. When you see "Fuselage Frames—Sta. 90.00," you know that the frame is 90 inches aft the nose. The reference datum is usually taken from the nose or zero station of the aircraft; sometimes, however, it is taken from the firewall.

The same station system is used for wing and stabilizer frames. The measurement is taken from the center line, or zero station, of the aircraft. Station numbers for a typical aircraft are shown in figure 2-3.

### MATERIAL SPECIFICATIONS

When working from prints you should ALWAYS USE THE MATERIAL SPECIFIED. NEVER make a substitution unless you have the proper authorization. The material indicated was selected by an engineer because it meets the requirements of the job. It is the best material for that particular part. Only an engineer or a person having the authority of an engineer for a particular piece of work can authorize substitutions of material when the kind specified is not available.

### HEAT TREATMENT

Practically all metals require some form of heat treatment in a manufacturing process. The title block on a blueprint, drawing, or specification lists the type of heat treatment required. Frequently it is necessary to remove the temper

from a piece of metal, in order that it may be machined to specifications, after which it must be retempered or hardened. Reference should be made to the heat treatment specifications in the title block, to determine the type required and the point during processing at which heat treatment is to occur.

### BILL OF MATERIAL

A special block or box on the drawing may contain a list of the pieces of stock necessary to make a part of an assembly of several parts. It is called a BILL OF MATERIAL or SCHEDULE (fig. 2-4) and indicates the type of stock, the size and the specific amount required.

The bill of material often contains a list of standard parts, known as a parts list or schedule. Many commonly used items, such as machine bolts, screws, turnbuckles, rivets, pipefittings, valves, and so on, have been standardized by the Navy, Army, and the Air Force.

### APPLICATION OR USAGE BLOCK

A usage block may be used to identify, by their drawing numbers, the larger units of which the detail part of subassembly shown on the drawing forms a component. This block is usually located near the title block, or it may form a part of the list of the bill of material. The general purpose of the USAGE or APPLICATION block is to provide a means for determining the equipment in which the part or assembly shown on the drawing is used. This block reveals the parts and assemblies that have a diversity of uses, and it aids in determining the effects of a change in the part or assembly shown on the drawing (fig. 2-5). See also figure 2-2.

### FINISH MARKS

Finish marks ( $\checkmark$ ) (illustrated in fig. 2-2) are used to indicate surfaces that must be finished by machining. Machining provides a better surface appearance and provides the fit with closely mated parts. In manufacturing, during the finishing process the required limits and tolerances must be observed. MACHINED FINISHES should not be confused with finishes of paint, enamel, grease, chromium plating, and similar coating.

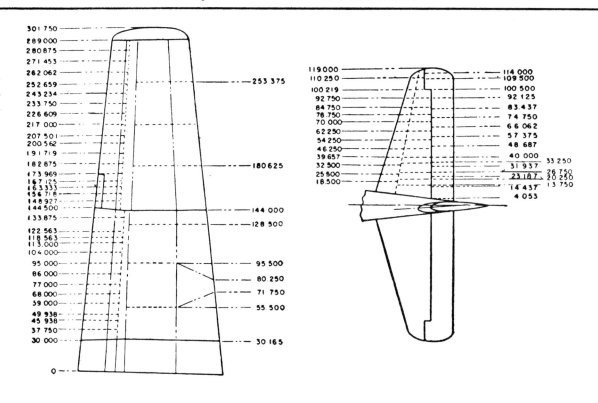

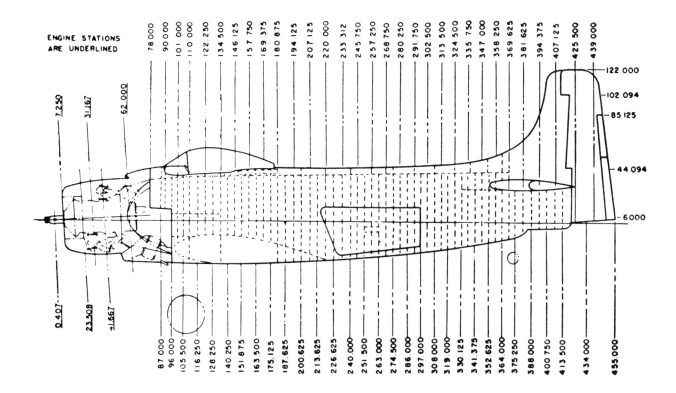

Figure 2-3.—Aircraft stations and frames.

## BILL OF MATERIAL

| ITEM NO. | DESCRIPTION | UNIT | ASSEMBLY OR SNS NO. | TROP | NORTH |
|---|---|---|---|---|---|
| 1 | BUILDING, 40' x 100' | EA | 1053 | 1 | - |
| 2 | BUILDING, 40' x 100' | EA | 2063 | - | 1 |
| 3 | PARTITION ASSEMBLY W/OUT DOOR | EA | 1406 | 1 | 1 |
| 4 | PARTITION ASSEMBLY W/DOOR | EA | 1407 | 1 | 1 |
| 7 | RECEPTACLE CIRCUIT | EA | 3017 | 1 | 1 |
| 8 | LIGHTING CIRCUIT | EA | 3022 | 1 | 1 |
| 9 | CABLE 2/C 9IN NONMETALLIC SHEATHED | LIN FT | 615-C-29705 | 500 | 500 |
| 11 | PORTABLE HANDLIGHT | EA | 617-C-29800 | 2 | 2 |
| 12 | FUSE, CARTRIDGE, 30 AMP, 230 V | EA | 617-F-15550-30 | 6 | 6 |
| 13 | FUSE, CARTRIDGE, 60 AMP | EA | 617-F-15557 | 6 | 6 |
| 14 | FUSES, PLUG, 30 AMP, 125 V | EA | 617-F-10400 | 16 | 16 |
| 15 | LINK, FUSE, RENEWABLE, 30 AMP, 230 V | EA | 617-F-17035 | 6 | 6 |
| 16 | LINK, FUSE, RENEWABLE, 60 AMP | EA | 617-F-17041 | 6 | 6 |
| 17 | LAMP, 60 WATTS, 120 V | EA | 617-L-3145 | 30 | 30 |
| 18 | REFLECTOR, CONE I/WEATHERPROOF SOCKET, 12" | EA | 617-R-5192 | 30 | 30 |
| 19 | SOCKET, LAMP, NO PULL CH, SCREW B, THPULITE, 250 V | EA | 617-S-10045-250 | 30 | 30 |
| 20 | LAMPHOLDER, WHOCR 40-106 | EA | 617-S-10045-400 | 30 | 30 |
| 21 | STRAP, CABLE | EA | 617-S-10500 | 300 | 300 |
| 22 | SWITCH, SAFETY, 3 POLE, 60 AMP | EA | 617-S-29663 | 1 | 1 |
| 24 | SWITCH, SAFETY, 2 PST, 30 AMP, 125/250 PLUG, FUSE TYPE | EA | 717-S-29674 | 6 | 6 |
| 25 | LUMBER, 1" x 2" RESAWN 1" x 4" | BF | | | |
| 26 | " 1" x 4" | BF | 630-L-40900-6010 | 1567 | 1567 |
| 27 | " 1" x 6" (16' L) | BF | 630-L-40940-6030 | 196 | 196 |
| 28 | " 2" x 4" | BF | 630-L-40845-6050 | 1100 | 1100 |
| 29 | " 2" x 6" | BF | 630-L-40841-6070 | 630 | 630 |
| 30 | " 2" x 8" | BF | 630-L-40841-6090 | 416 | 416 |
| 31 | " 2" x 10" | BF | 630-L-40845-6110 | 2120 | 2120 |
| 33 | " 4" x 4" | BF | 630-L-40845-6970 | 137 | 137 |
| 34 | " 1" x 6" T & G (12' L) | BF | 630-L-40720 | 82 | 82 |
| 35 | " 2" x 4" T & G (12' L) | BF | 630-L-40730 | 5400 | 5400 |
| 36 | MOULD, LABEL, 1-1/16" x 1-5/8" | LIN FT | 730-M-307-100 | 2900 | 2900 |
| 38 | PLYWOOD, 3/4" THICK, MOISTURE RESISTANT | SQ FT | 530-P-16004-1010 | 5056 | 5056 |
| 39 | " 1/2" " " | SQ FT | 530-P-16004-1510 | 3204 | 3204 |
| 40 | NAILS, 4d | LB | 042-N-21804 | 110 | 110 |
| 41 | NAILS, 6d (COMMON WIRE) | LB | 042-N-25008 | 100 | 100 |
| 42 | " 8d | LB | 042-N-25012 | 50 | 50 |
| 43 | " 10d | LB | 042-N-25016 | 200 | 200 |
| 44 | " 16d | LB | 042-N-25420 | 35 | 35 |
| 45 | MESH, WIRE, 6" x 6" #6 GAUGE | SQ FT | 042-W-4005 | 4000 | 4000 |
| 46 | SCREW ANCHOR, 3/8 x 2" | EA | 043-A-1715-210 | 300 | 300 |
| 47 | SHIELD, EXPANSION, 5/8" x 3-1/2" F/LAG SCREW | EA | 043-A-1715-250 | 78 | 78 |
| 48 | BOLT, MACHINE, 3/8" x 6" | EA | 043-B-70029-609 | 130 | 130 |
| 49 | BOLT, MACHINE, 1/2" x 10" | EA | 043-B-70029-4226 | 52 | 52 |
| 50 | SCREW, LAG, 3/8"B x 4" | EA | 043-S-630H | 790 | 790 |
| 51 | " 5/8"B x 4" | EA | 043-S-6040 | 78 | 78 |
| 52 | " METAL #8 1" R.H. | 000 | 043-S-10000-200 | 2 | 2 |
| 53 | " #8 3/4" R.H. TYPE A | 000 | 043-S-10000-400 | 2 | 2 |
| 55 | WASHER, FOR 3/8"B BOLT | LB | 043-W-4012 | 5 | 5 |
| 56 | ANGLE, 3" x 3" x 5/16" | LB | 046-A-1300 | 230 | 230 |
| 57 | CEMENT, PORTLAND IN EXPORT BAGS | BAG | 050-C-323 | 25 | 25 |
| 58 | FIBER BOARD, 1/2" THICK, HARD PRESSED | SQ FT | 050-F-330-20 | 804 | 804 |
| | WASHER FOR 1/2" BOLT | LB | 043-W-4028 | 4 | 4 |
| 59 | NUT, HX, NC, 3/8" | EA | 643-N-6072 | 135 | 135 |
| 60 | NUT, HX, NC, 1/2" | EA | 643-N-6078 | 55 | 99 |

**Figure 2-4.—A bill of material (Schedule).**

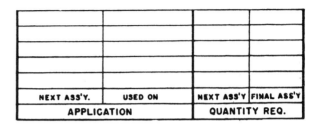

| | | | |
|---|---|---|---|
| | | | |
| | | | |
| | | | |
| | | | |
| | | | |
| NEXT ASS'Y. | USED ON | NEXT ASS'Y | FINAL ASS'Y |
| APPLICATION | | QUANTITY REQ. | |

**Figure 2-5.—Application or usage blocks.**

## NOTES AND SPECIFICATIONS

Blueprints contain all the information about an object or part which can be presented graphically (that is, in drawing). A considerable amount of information can be presented this way, but there is more information required by supervisors, contractors, manufacturers, and craftsmen, which is not adaptable to the graphic form of presentation. Information of this type is generally given on the drawings as notes or as a set of specifications attached to the drawings.

NOTES are generally placed on drawings to give additional information to clarify the object on the blueprint. Leader lines are used to indicate the precise part being notated.

A SPECIFICATION is a statement or document containing a description or enumeration of particulars, as the terms of a contract, or details of an object or objects not shown on a blueprint or drawing.

Specifications (specs) are normally attached to a set of blueprints to: describe items so that they may be procured, assembled and maintained to function in accordance with the performance requirements; furnish sufficient information to permit determination of conformance to the description; and furnish the above in sufficient completeness for accomplishment without the need of research, development, design engineering, or help from the preparing organization.

## FEDERAL SPECIFICATIONS

Federal specifications cover the characteristics of material and supplies used jointly by the Navy and other Government departments.

All Federal specifications used by the Navy Department as purchase specifications are listed in the Department of Defense Index of Specifications and Standards.

## MILITARY (MIL AND JAN) SPECIFICATIONS

Coordinated military (MIL and JAN) specs are those which have been developed and approved by the Department of Defense for use in procurement of supplies and materials used by the Departments of the Army, the Navy, and the Air Force. These specs are identified by the letters "MIL" or "JAN" followed by the first letter of the material and a serial number. They are listed both alphabetically and numerically in the Department of Defense Index of Specifications and Standards.

### LEGENDS OR SYMBOLS

The legend is generally placed in the upper right corner of a blueprint, if space permits. The legend is used to explain or define a symbol or special mark placed on a blueprint. Figure 2-6 shows a legend for an electrical plan of a building.

### ALPHABET OF LINES

In order to be able to read blueprints you must acquire a knowledge of the use of lines. The alphabet of lines is the common language of the technician and the engineer. Just as a word in the spoken language requires letters of the alphabet to have meaning, the object on the blueprint requires several different types of lines in order to impart information to the reader of the blueprint.

### OUTLINE LINES

The outline lines are thick solid lines that represent the edges and surfaces that are visible from the angle at which the original drawing was made.

### CENTER LINES

The center lines are thin lines composed of long and short dashes, alternately and evenly spaced with a long dash at each end. The center lines signify the center of a circle or arc, and are also used to divide drawings into equal or symmetrical parts. Center lines are always used to locate the center of any hollowed part of an object.

### HIDDEN LINES

Hidden lines are medium lines which consist of short dashes evenly spaced. They show the hidden features of a part. Figure 2-7 illustrates the use of all the lines mentioned in this chapter.

### DIMENSION LINES

Dimension lines are thin lines which indicate the size of objects on a blueprint. There are two methods of showing dimensions on a blueprint; one is by reading the dimension that is placed in the break of the dimension line, and the other is a dimension line without a break terminated by arrows, with the dimension shown above the line. In either case, the dimension distance is read from the point of one arrowhead to the point of the other arrowhead.

### EXTENSION LINES

Extension lines are thin lines which indicate the extent of a dimension and will always be touched by the point of the arrowhead of a dimension line.

### LEADERS

Leaders are thin lines used to indicate a part or portion to which a number, note or other information refers, and are always terminated with an arrowhead. See figure 2-7.

### CUTTING PLANE LINES

A cutting plane is a thick line which indicates the path of the object that is cut to show a section. Referring to figure 2-7, you will note that the cutting plane line has the arrowheads pointing to the left. The section view to the right (section A-A) is to be viewed looking in the direction in which the arrowheads are pointing.

### PHANTOM LINES

Phantom lines are medium lines used to indicate the alternate position of parts of the item delineated, repeated detail, or the relative position of an absent part. In figure 2-7 the phantom lines are used to show the relative position of an absent part.

## LEGEND:

| | |
|---|---|
| O₈ | FLUORESCENT FIXTURE, 8 DENOTES |
| 50 | CIRCUIT NUMBER, #50 DENOTES TYPE |
| ⊸⊹⊢ | HOMERUN, 3 -#12 WIRE IN ½" CONDUIT UNLESS OTHERWISE NOTED, ¾"CONDUIT IN FLOOR |
| ⊕ | DUPLEX RECEPTACLE |
| S | SWITCH |
| S₃ | 3 WAY SWITCH |
| - - - - | CONDUIT IN FLOOR |
| ——— | CONDUIT IN CEILING |
| O No.11 | OUTLET BOX, FIXTURE No.11 TO BE INSTALLED |
| Ⓧ | EXIT LIGHT |
| ⊗F | FLOOD LIGHT |
| ⋈ | FIRE ALARM SIREN |
| ⊲⊐ | BELL - 4 INCH, 110 V. VIBRATING TYPE |
| Ⓒ | CLOCK OUTLET |
| Ⓣ | THERMOSTAT |
| J̄ | JUNCTION BOX |
| ∝ | FAN, TOILET ROOMS |
| ℚ | MOTOR CONNECTION |
| ▼ | TELEPHONE OUTLET |
| ⚬⚬ᴾᴹ | PLUG IN MOULDING |
| 🔲 | FIRE ALARM SWITCH 110V. |
| 🔲 | 110V. PUSH BUTTON FOR BELLS |

| FIXTURE# | PLATE #(9Y9) | WATTAGE |
|---|---|---|
| 5 | 2 | 100 W |
| 7 | 2 | 2-25W |
| 11 | 2 (WITH WALL SWITCH) | 60W |
| 23 | 5 | 60W |
| 25 | 5 | 100W |
| 28 | 5 | 100W |
| 50 | (SPEC.) | 2-40W |
| 51 | (SPEC.) | 150 W |

NOTE: SEE SPECIFICATIONS FOR DETAILED
INFORMATION ON LIGHTING FIXTURES

FLUORESCENT LIGHT DETAIL
NO SCALE
FIXTURE 50, 2 40W

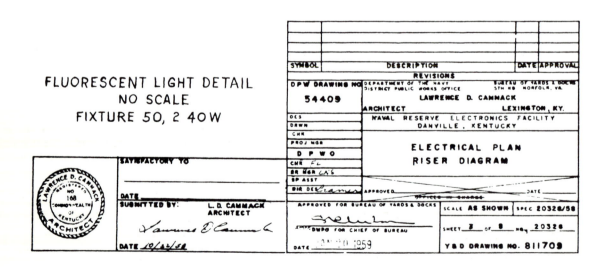

Figure 2-6.—An electrical plan (note the legend).

BREAK LINES ——————

The LONG BREAK LINE simply indicates that a part or object has been shortened, it is merely a space saver for the draftsman; it does not change the actual length indicated by the dimension.

The SHORT BREAK LINE indicates that the draftsman has removed part of an outer surface to reveal the inside structure.

Break lines used to shorten metal rods, metal tubes, metal bars, and wood, are shown in figure 2-8; also shown are the long and short break lines.

## SCALES

Any graduated instrument or measuring stick used to measure distance or length may be called a scale, but technically the graduations themselves are the scale. Scales are made in a wide variety of shapes, sizes and materials, and for many purposes.

Because the space of a drawing sheet does not permit objects to be shown in their actual dimensions (true size), dimensions in accurate proportion to actual dimensions of the objects are used. Large objects must be drawn to a reduced size or very small objects must be drawn to an enlarged size. The scale provides the draftsman with an instrument which enables him to lay out on the drawing proportional dimensions quickly and easily.

### ARCHITECTS' SCALE

Architects' Scales (fig. 2-9) are divided into proportional feet and inches and are generally used in scaling drawings for machine and structural work. The triangular architects' scale usually contains 11 scales, each subdivided differently. Six scales read from the left end, while five scales read from the right end. Figure 2-9 shows how the 3/16-inch subdivision of the architects' scale is further subdivided into 12 equal parts representing 1 inch each, and the 3/32-inch subdivision into 6 equal parts representing 2 inches each.

### ENGINEERS' SCALES

Engineers' Scales (fig. 2-9) are divided into decimal graduations (10, 20, 30, 40, 50, and 60 divisions to the inch). These scales are used for plotting and map drawing and in the graphic solution of problems.

### METRIC SCALES

Metric Scales (fig. 2-9) are used in conjunction with drawings, maps and so forth, made in countries using the metric system. This system is also being used with increasing frequency in the United States. The scale is divided into centimeters and millimeters. In conversion, 2.54 cm (centimeters) are equal to 1 inch.

### GRAPHIC SCALES

Graphic Scales (fig. 2-9) are lines subdivided into distances corresponding to convenient units of length on the ground or of the object represented by the blueprint. They are placed in or near the title block of the drawing and their relative lengths to the scales of the drawing are not affected if the print is reduced or enlarged.

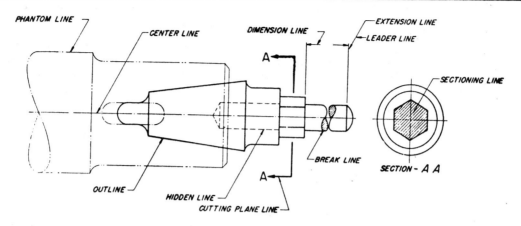

Figure 2-7. —Line conventions.

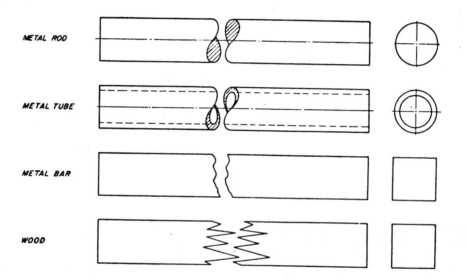

Figure 2-8. —Break lines.

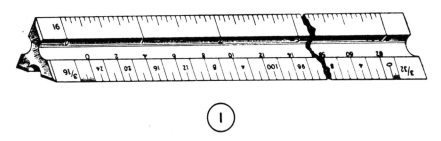

**①**

## ARCHITECTS' SCALE

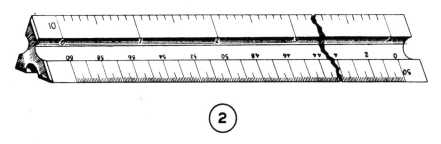

**②**

## ENGINEERS' SCALE

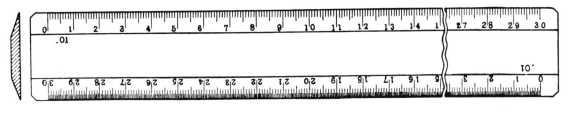

**③**

## METRIC SCALE

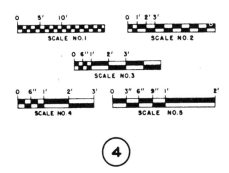

**④**

## GRAPHIC SCALES

Figure 2-9.—Types of scales.

# CHAPTER 3

# READING PROJECTION AND SPECIAL VIEWS

In learning to read blueprints you must develop the ability to visualize the object (fig. 3-1) by properly interpreting the various types of lines, dimensions, sections, details, symbols, views, and other media used by the designer or draftsman in drawing an object or parts of an object to be utilized by a craftsman or engineer.

You probably did some visualizing when you planned your last long road trip. You consulted a road map to find the best roads to your destination, the approximate distance, the direction, and so on. These were indicated on the map by various widths and colors of lines and symbols. You did not actually see the roads, you knew by checking the colors and symbols that the relatively wide red lines were primary roads. Two red lines side by side were dual highways, dark blue lines were secondary roads, light blue lines were creeks, sky blue areas were marked as lakes and river, and so on. Basically the same techniques used to read a road map, can be applied to reading a blueprint.

## ORTHOGRAPHIC VIEWS

Prints that furnish complete information for construction and repair present an object in its true proportions. These prints are accurate and indicate true shape and size. These prints are usually drawn by ORTHOGRAPHIC PROJECTION, a parallel projection in which the projectors are perpendicular to the plane of projection.

The number of views to be used in projecting a drawing is governed by the complexity of the shape of the drawing. Complex drawings are normally drawn showing six views; that is both ends, front, top, rear, and bottom (fig. 3-2). Figure 3-2 shows an object placed in a transparent box hinged at the edges. The projections on the sides of the box are the views seen by looking straight at the object through each side. If the outlines are scribed on each surface and the box opened as shown and laid flat, the result is a 6-view, orthographic projection drawing. It should be noted, also, that the rear plane may be considered hinged to either of the side planes or to the top or bottom plane; thus the rear view may be shown in any one of four positions (to the right of the right side view or left of the left side view, above the top view or below the bottom view). As a general rule you will find that most drawings will be presented in three views. Occasionally you will see 2-view drawings, particularly cylindrical objects.

## 3-VIEW DRAWINGS

A 3-view orthographic projection drawing generally shows the FRONT, TOP, and RIGHT SIDE view of an object. Refer back to figure 3-2 and note the position of the front, top, and right side view; by eliminating the rear, bottom, and left side view, the drawing is changed from a 6-view drawing to a conventional 3-view drawing.

Figure 3-1.—Visualizing a blueprint.

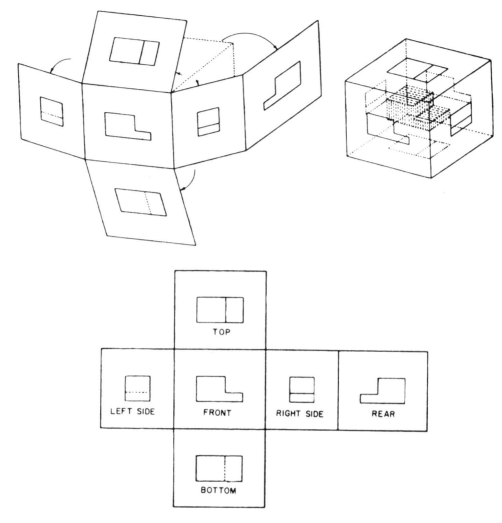

Figure 3-2.—Third-angle orthographic projection.

Study the arrangement of the three views shown in figure 3-3. The front view is the starting point. It was selected as the front view because it shows the most characteristic feature of the object—the notch.

The right side or end view is projected to the right of the front view. Note that all the horizontal outlines of the front view are extended horizontally to make up the side view. After you study each view of the object, you should be able to visualize the object as it appears in figure 3-4. In order to clarify the 3-view drawing further, think of the object as being immovable (fig. 3-5), and that you are moving around it. This will help you to relate the blueprint views to the appearance of the object concerned.

In summarizing the visualization of the object shown in figures 3-3, 3-4, and 3-5, you should

have obtained the following knowledge about the object: the shape of the object, the overall length of the object which is 2 1/8 inches, and its width 1 1/2 inches. The object is 1 3/8 inches high, and is notched 1 1/8 inches from the right side and 7/8 inch from the bottom.

To take you one step further, study the 3-view drawing illustrated in figure 3-6. Note that in this illustration the shape of the object is similar to that shown in figure 3-3, with one exception; the object in figure 3-6 has a 1/2-inch hole drilled in the notched portion of the object. This drawing is read in the same manner as the other 3-view drawing. The hidden lines shown on the front view of the drawing tell you the exact location of the walls of this hole (1/2 inch). The hidden lines are also shown on the side view. You must remember, in viewing this object

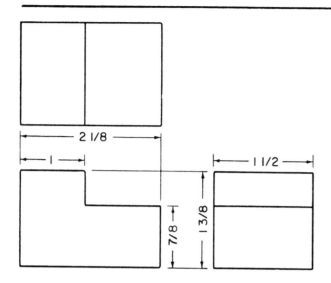

Figure 3-3.—The orthographic views.

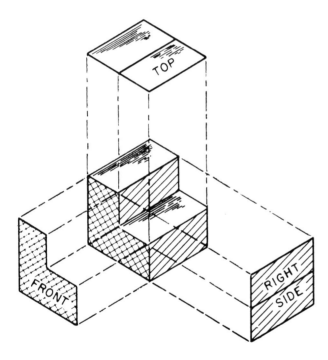

Figure 3-4.—Pull off the views.

from the front, the drilled hole is not visible; that is the reason for the hidden lines. This is also true in looking from the right side.

The 3-view drawing shown in figure 3-6 introduces two more symbols from the "alphabet of lines" that are not shown in figure 3-3: the hidden line, and the center line which gives

Figure 3-5.—Compare the orthographic views with the model.

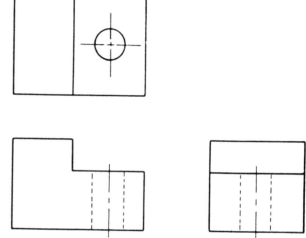

Figure 3-6.—A three view drawing.

the location of the exact center of the drilled hole. The shape and size of the object are the same.

As a test of your ability to visualize and interpret simple 3-view drawings, answer the following questions pertaining to figure 3-7. The answers are given at the end of this chapter.

QUESTIONS ON THE JIG BLOCK

Refer to figure 3-7.
1. What is the overall height of the jig block?
2. What is the overall width of the jig block?

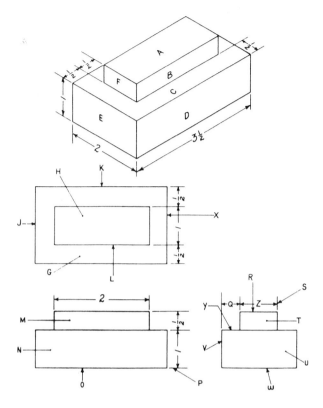

Figure 3-7.—Jig block.

3. What is the overall length of the jig block?
4. What surface in the top view represents A?
5. What kind of lines are J, O, W, X, Y and V?
6. Surface D is represented by what letter in the front view?
7. F is represented by what letter in the side view.
8. What is the dimension of Z?
9. What is the diemsnion of Q?
10. What type of lines are Q and Z?
11. What kind of lines are P and S?
12. Surface B is represented by what surface in the front view?
13. Surface C is represented by what surface in the top view?
14. What is the width of surface H?
15. What is the length of surface M?
16. Surface E is represented by what surface on the side view?
17. Surface B is represented by what letter in the top view?

18. How many jig blocks are to be made?
19. What type of metal is the jig block to be made off?
20. What letter or letters denote(s) extension line(s)?
21. What letters in the top view denote outlines or visible lines?

## PICTORIAL DRAWINGS

The purpose of a pictorial drawing is to show general location, function, and appearance of parts and assemblies. There are three common types of pictorial views drawn by draftsmen: (1) the isometric, (2) the oblique (cavalier and cabinet), and (3) the perspective.

## ISOMETRIC

The isometric drawing is the most commonly used and the most useful in making freehand sketches.

In an isometric drawing, all lines that are parallel on the object are also parallel on the drawing. Vertical lines are shown in a vertical position, but lines representing horizontal lines are drawn at an angle of 30° with the horizontal. Also, on an isometric drawing, all the lines which represent the horizontal and vertical lines on an object have true length. Since all isometric lines are spread equally (120°) - the same scale of measure is used on the 3 visible sides. Isometric drawings (fig. 3-8) may be dimensioned, and blueprints of these drawings may be used for making simple objects. But, isometric drawings cannot be used alone for complicated parts or structures. Isometric drawings may be used as an aid in clarifying the orthographic drawings that are the foundation of all construction blueprints.

## OBLIQUE

In an oblique drawing, the front face of the object is shown in its true size and shape as if it were an orthographic (6- or 3-view) drawing, and the receding lines of the other two sides shown, are drawn obliquely at any angle, usually 30°, 45°, or 60° to the horizontal (fig. 3-9). Measuring scale for the oblique sides may be any selected scale to give the object realistic depth (normally 3/4 the scale of the front view).

CABINET DRAWING (fig. 3-10) is an oblique drawing with a special name because it is often

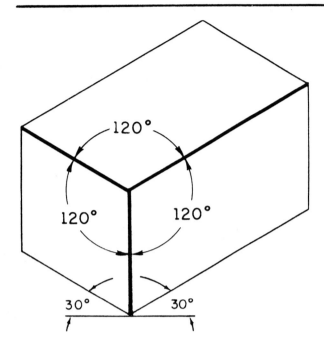

Figure 3-8.—Isometric drawing.

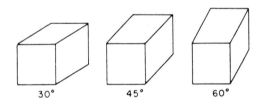

Figure 3-9.—Oblique views of a rectangular block.

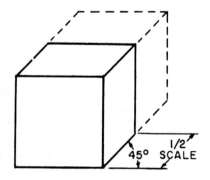

Figure 3-10.—A cabinet drawing of a cube.

used for drawings of cabinet work. It is distinguished by the use of 1/2 scale measurements on the oblique sides, compared to full scale measurements on the front plane. Cabinet drawings are commonly drawn with the oblique sides at 30° or 45°.

A CAVALIER DRAWING (fig. 3-11) is another special type of oblique projection wherein the receding or oblique planes are drawn to the same scale as that used on the front plane. This creates a drawing distorted from the object's true proportions, but allows the use of one scale of measure for the entire drawing. Cavalier drawings are drawn with the oblique planes 45° to the front plane.

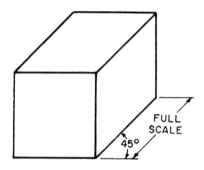

Figure 3-11.—A cavalier drawing of a cube.

PERSPECTIVE

The most truly pictorial method of presentation is perspective drawing. By this method, objects are made to appear proportionately smaller with distance just as they do when you look at them (fig. 3-12). However, perspective drawings are difficult to draw and, since lines on perspective drawings are drawn in diminishing proportion to the edges represented, a perspective drawing cannot be used when an object is to be constructed. It is of value chiefly for illustrative purposes, particularly for technical illustration in the commercial and architectural fields.

Note the differences among the isometric, oblique, the cavalier, and the cabinet drawing shown in figure 3-13.

SPECIAL VIEWS

In many complex objects it is often difficult for the draftsmen to show true size and shapes of an object orthographically. Therefore, the

Figure 3-12.—The perspective.

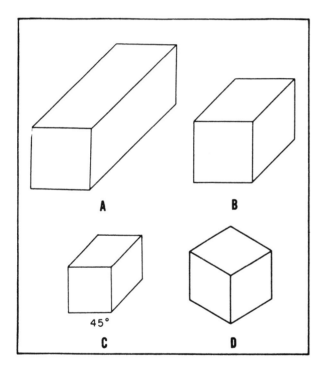

Figure 3-13.—A. Cavalier drawing. B. Cabinet drawing. C. Oblique drawing. D. Isometric drawing.

draftsmen must use other media to give the engineer and craftsman a clear picture of the object to be constructed. Among these media are auxiliary views, rotations, details, section views, phantom views, exploded views, and

developments. These special views will be covered in this chapter.

## AUXILIARY VIEWS

Auxiliary views are often necessary to clearly show the true shape and length of inclined surfaces, or other features which are not parallel to any of the principal planes of projection.

Look directly at the front view of figure 3-14. Notice the inclined surface. Now look at the right side view and top view. The inclined surface appears foreshortened—not its true shape or size. For a case like this the draftsman will use the auxiliary view to show the true shape and size of the inclined face of the object. It is obtained by looking directly at the inclined surface. The principle of the auxiliary view is illustrated in figure 3-15.

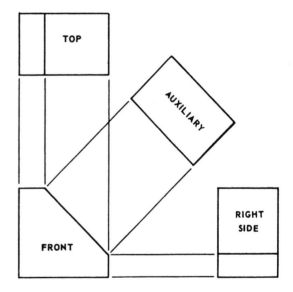

Figure 3-14.—Auxiliary view arrangement.

If you would reflect for a moment back to figure 3-5 showing the immovable object being viewed from the front, top and side to obtain the three orthographic views, and compare it with figure 3-16, together with the other information, it should clearly explain the reading of the auxiliary view. For a side by side comparison of an orthographic view and an auxiliary projection, see figure 3-17. You will see a foreshortened orthographic view in figure 3-17A of the inclined or slanted surface whose true

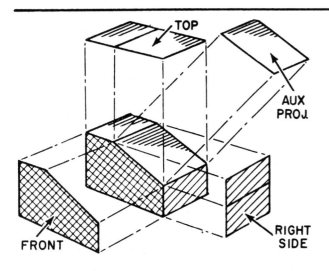

Figure 3-15.—Auxiliary projection principle.

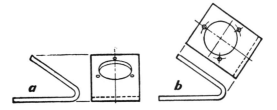

Figure 3-17.—Comparison of orthographic and auxiliary projection.

size and shape are shown projected as an auxiliary projection in figure 3-17B.

## ROTATION

The projection of the auxiliary view as mentioned earlier is obtained by the observer moving around an immovable object, and the views projected perpendicular to the lines of sight. Remember, the object has not been moved, only the position of the viewer has been changed.

In a ROTATION view the object is moved (rotated), while the viewer remains stationary.

Figure 3-18 illustrates a 2-view orthographic view (A), an auxiliary view (B), and a rotation view (C) of an object. To clarify the rotation principle, an extra top view has been inserted (circled) to show the object rotated on its center axis and the right portion, from the center line of the object, has been projected in the front view. In short, the rotation view is similar to taking the auxiliary view (B), and placing it horizontally against the front view (B).

## PHANTOM VIEWS

PHANTOM views are used to indicate the alternate position of parts of the item drawn, repeated detail, or the relative position of an absent part. Figure 3-19 shows a phantom view of a part in the alternate position (the part to the left of the figure made up of one long line and two short dashes).

## SECTIONS

Section views are used to give a clearer view of the interior or hidden feature of an object which normally cannot be clearly observed in conventional outside views.

A section view is obtained by cutting away part of an object to show the shape and construction at the cutting plane.

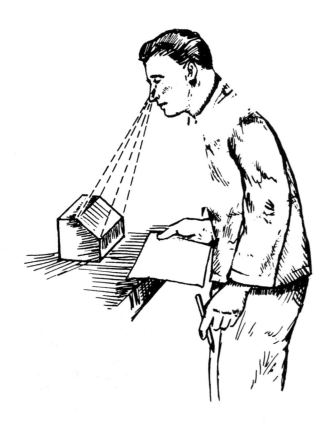

Figure 3-16.—Viewing an inclined surface, auxiliary view.

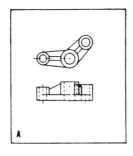 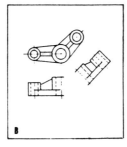 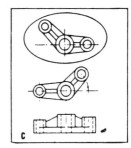

Figure 3-18.—Rotation and auxiliary views compared.

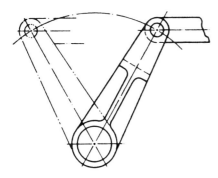

Figure 3-19.—Phantom view showing
alternative position.

Notice the CUTTING PLANE LINE AA in figure 3-20A. It shows where the imaginary cut has been made. The isometric view in figure 3-20B helps you to visualize the cutting plane. The arrows point in the direction in which you are to look at the sectional view.

Figure 3-20C is a front showing how the object would look if it were cut in half.

The orthographic section view of section A-A, figure 3-20D, is placed on the drawing instead of the confusing front view in figure 3-20A. Notice how much easier it is to read and understand.

When sectional views are drawn, the part that is cut by the cutting plane is marked with diagonal, parallel SECTION LINES. The draftsmen's word for the process of making these lines is crosshatching. When two or more parts are shown in one view, each part is sectioned or crosshatched with a different slant of line. Section views are necessary for a clear understanding of complicated parts. On simple drawings, a section may serve the purpose of an additional view.

Section A-A in figure 3-20D is known as a FULL SECTION because the object is cut completely through.

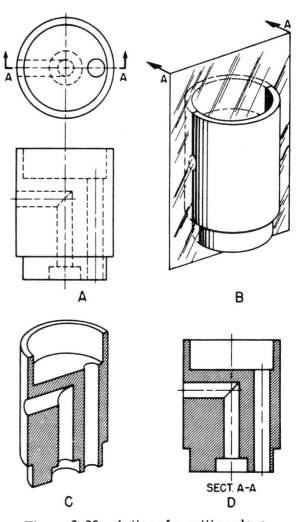

Figure 3-20.—Action of a cutting plane.

## Offset Section

A section view which has the cutting plane changing direction backward and forward (zig-zag), so as to pass through features that are important to show, is known as an OFFSET SECTION. The offset cutting plane in figure 3-21 is arranged so that the hole on the right side will be shown in section. The sectional view is the front view, and the top views show the offset cutting plane line.

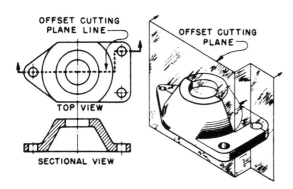

Figure 3-21.—Offset section.

## Half Section

Figure 3-22 shows a HALF SECTION. A half section is normally used when the object is symmetrical in both outside and inside details. One-half of the object is sectioned; the outer half is shown as a standard view.

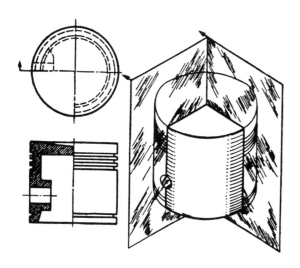

Figure 3-22.—Half section.

The object is round, and if it were cut into two equal parts and then those parts divided equally, you would have four quarters. Now remove a quarter. This is what the cutting plane has done in the pictorial view. A quarter of the cylinder has been removed so that you can look inside. If the cutting plane had extended along the diameter of the cylinder, you would have been looking at a full section. But the cutting plane in this drawing extends the distance of the radius, or only half the distance of a full section. Hence it is called a half section.

The arrow has been inserted to show your line of sight. What you see from that point is drawn as a half section in the orthographic view. The width of the orthographic view represents the diameter of the circle. One radius is shown as a half section, the other as an external view.

## Revolved Section

To eliminate drawing extra views of rolled shapes, ribs, and similar forms, the draftsman uses a REVOLVED SECTION. It is really a drawing within a drawing, and it clearly describes the object's shape at a certain cross-section station or point.

The draftsman has revolved the sectional view of the rib in figure 3-23 so that you can look at it head-on. Because of this revolving feature, this kind of section is called a revolved section.

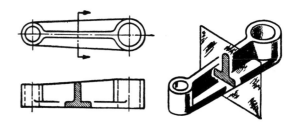

Figure 3-23.—Revolved section.

## Removed Section

REMOVED SECTIONS are normally used to illustrate particular parts of an object. They are drawn like the revolved section, except that they are placed at one side to bring out important details. They are often drawn to a larger scale than the view on which they are indicated (fig. 3-24).

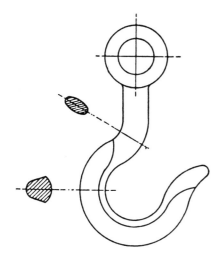

Figure 3-24.—Removed section.

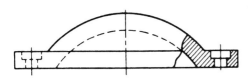

Figure 3-25.—Broken-out section through a counterbored hole.

## Broken Out Section

The inner structure of a small area may be shown by peeling back or removing the outside surface. The inside of the counterbored hole is better illustrated in figure 3-25 because of the BROKEN-OUT SECTION, which makes it possible for you to "look inside."

## Aligned Section

Look at the front view of the handwheel in figure 3-26. Notice the cutting plane line AA.

When a true sectional view might be misleading, parts such as ribs or spokes are drawn as if they are rotated into or out of the cutting plane. Notice that the spokes in the section at A-A are not sectioned. In some cases, though not in this figure, if the spokes were sectioned, the first impression would be that the wheel had a solid web rather than spokes.

## EXPLODED VIEWS

Another special type of view, which is very helpful and easy to read, is the EXPLODED VIEW. The exploded view is used to show rela-

tive location of parts; it is particularly helpful in assembling complex objects. Notice how parts are spread out in line to show clearly each part's relationship to the other parts (fig. 3-27).

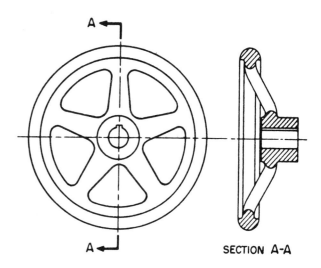

Figure 3-26.—Aligned section.

Figure 3-27.—An exploded view.

## DEVELOPMENTS

Development is the method a layout man uses to make a flat pattern which can be transferred to sheet metal and formed into a curved or angular form. The Shipfitter (M) and the Steelworker (F) do a great deal of this but men of most ratings will benefit by knowing even a little something about development from a blueprint reading point of view.

In figure 3-28A you will see a pictorial view of a sheet metal cone. As the cone has no bottom, we can look into it and see the joint which has purposely been left open for this illustration. To find out how the development or pattern for this cone would look, see figure 3-28B. The length of the side of the cone (not the height from base to top) is represented on the development as L. The circumference of the base of the cone is represented by the curved dimension line and the letter C. The stretchout, B in the figure (stretchout is another name used interchangeably with pattern or development), when rolled up, would give you the cone shown in A. Likewise, you could transfer the stretchout to sheet metal, run the metal through a slip roll forming machine, and you would have a sheet metal cone.

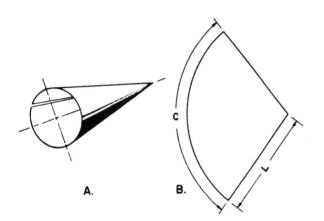

Figure 3-28.—Sheet metal cone.

ANSWERS TO QUESTIONS ON JIG BLOCK

1. 1 1/2"
2. 2"
3. 3 1/2"
4. H
5. Outline or visible lines
6. N
7. T
8. 1"
9. 1/2"
10. Dimension lines
11. Extension lines
12. M
13. G
14. 1"
15. 2"
16. U
17. L
18. 7
19. Cold rolled steel
20. S and P
21. J, K, and L.

# ANSWER SHEET

TEST NO. _____ PART _____ TITLE OF POSITION _____
(AS GIVEN IN EXAMINATION ANNOUNCEMENT - INCLUDE OPTION, IF ANY)

PLACE OF EXAMINATION _____ DATE_____
(CITY OR TOWN)                                    (STATE)

RATING

## USE THE SPECIAL PENCIL.   MAKE GLOSSY BLACK MARKS.

Make only ONE mark for each answer.   Additional and stray marks may be
counted as mistakes.   In making corrections, erase errors COMPLETELY.

# ANSWER SHEET

T NO. _____ PART _____ TITLE OF POSITION _____

(AS GIVEN IN EXAMINATION ANNOUNCEMENT - INCLUDE OPTION, IF ANY)

CE OF EXAMINATION _____ DATE _____

(CITY OR TOWN)　　　　　　　　　　(STATE)

RATING

USE THE SPECIAL PENCIL.　MAKE GLOSSY BLACK MARKS.

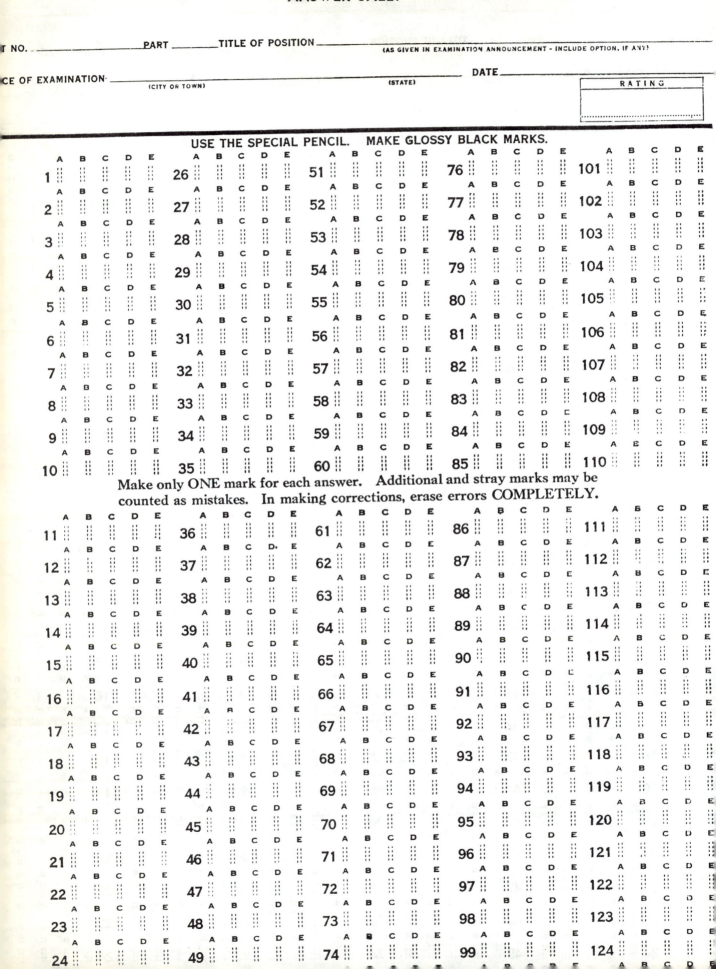

Make only ONE mark for each answer.　Additional and stray marks may be counted as mistakes.　In making corrections, erase errors COMPLETELY.

3576